Advancing Commercialization of Digital Products from Federal Laboratories

Committee on Advancing Commercialization from the Federal Laboratories

Board on Science, Technology, and Economic Policy

Policy and Global Affairs

A Consensus Study Report of
The National Academies of
SCIENCES • ENGINEERING • MEDICINE

THE NATIONAL ACADEMIES PRESS
Washington, DC
www.nap.edu

THE NATIONAL ACADEMIES PRESS 500 Fifth Street, NW Washington, DC 20001

This activity was supported by a contract between the National Academy of Sciences and the National Institute of Standards and Technology (SB134117CQ0017/1333ND18FNB400154). Any opinions, findings, conclusions, or recommendations expressed in this publication do not necessarily reflect the views of any organization or agency that provided support for the project.

International Standard Book Number-13: 978-0-309-68594-8
International Standard Book Number-10: 0-309-68594-X
Digital Object Identifier: https://doi.org/10.17226/26006

Additional copies of this publication are available from the National Academies Press, 500 Fifth Street, NW, Keck 360, Washington, DC 20001; (800) 624-6242 or (202) 334-3313; http://www.nap.edu.

Copyright 2021 by the National Academy of Sciences. All rights reserved.

Printed in the United States of America

Suggested citation: National Academies of Sciences, Engineering, and Medicine. 2021. *Advancing Commercialization of Digital Products from Federal Laboratories*. Washington, DC: The National Academies Press. https://doi.org/10.17226/26006.

The National Academies of
SCIENCES • ENGINEERING • MEDICINE

The **National Academy of Sciences** was established in 1863 by an Act of Congress, signed by President Lincoln, as a private, nongovernmental institution to advise the nation on issues related to science and technology. Members are elected by their peers for outstanding contributions to research. Dr. Marcia McNutt is president.

The **National Academy of Engineering** was established in 1964 under the charter of the National Academy of Sciences to bring the practices of engineering to advising the nation. Members are elected by their peers for extraordinary contributions to engineering. Dr. John L. Anderson is president.

The **National Academy of Medicine** (formerly the Institute of Medicine) was established in 1970 under the charter of the National Academy of Sciences to advise the nation on medical and health issues. Members are elected by their peers for distinguished contributions to medicine and health. Dr. Victor J. Dzau is president.

The three Academies work together as the **National Academies of Sciences, Engineering, and Medicine** to provide independent, objective analysis and advice to the nation and conduct other activities to solve complex problems and inform public policy decisions. The National Academies also encourage education and research, recognize outstanding contributions to knowledge, and increase public understanding in matters of science, engineering, and medicine.

Learn more about the National Academies of Sciences, Engineering, and Medicine at **www.nationalacademies.org**.

The National Academies of
SCIENCES • ENGINEERING • MEDICINE

Consensus Study Reports published by the National Academies of Sciences, Engineering, and Medicine document the evidence-based consensus on the study's statement of task by an authoring committee of experts. Reports typically include findings, conclusions, and recommendations based on information gathered by the committee and the committee's deliberations. Each report has been subjected to a rigorous and independent peer-review process and it represents the position of the National Academies on the statement of task.

Proceedings published by the National Academies of Sciences, Engineering, and Medicine chronicle the presentations and discussions at a workshop, symposium, or other event convened by the National Academies. The statements and opinions contained in proceedings are those of the participants and are not endorsed by other participants, the planning committee, or the National Academies.

For information about other products and activities of the National Academies, please visit www.nationalacademies.org/about/whatwedo.

COMMITTEE ON ADVANCING COMMERCIALIZATION FROM THE FEDERAL LABORATORIES

Ruth L. Okediji, *Co-Chair*, Harvard Law School
Donald Siegel, *Co-Chair*, Arizona State University
Margo A. Bagley, Emory University School of Law
Mary Beth Campbell, California Institute of Technology
Wesley M. Cohen, Duke University
Mark S. Kamlet, Carnegie Mellon University
Arti Rai, Duke University School of Law
Joel Waldfogel, University of Minnesota
John Wilbanks, Sage Bionetworks
Jetta Wong, JLW Advising

STUDY STAFF
Gail Cohen, Study Director
David Dierksheide, Program Officer
Anita Eisenstadt, Program Officer
Frederic Lestina, Research Associate (through September 2020)
Clara Savage, Financial Officer

SUBJECT MATTER CONSULTANTS
Jorge L. Contreras, Senior Consultant
Jerome Reichman, Consultant

CONSULTANTS
Michael Baumer, Consultant
Honggi Lee, Consultant
Robert Samors, Consultant

BOARD ON SCIENCE, TECHNOLOGY, AND ECONOMIC POLICY

Adam B. Jaffe, *Chair*, Brandeis University
Noël Bakhtian, Lawrence Berkeley National Laboratory
Jeff Bingaman, Former U.S. Senator, New Mexico
Brenda J. Dietrich (NAE), Cornell University
Brian G. Hughes, HBN Shoe, LLC
Adriana Kugler, Georgetown University
Arati Prabhakar (NAE), Founder and CEO, Actuate
Paula E. Stephan, Georgia State University
Scott Stern, Massachusetts Institute of Technology
John C. Wall (NAE), Cummins, Inc. (Retired)
John L. Anderson (NAE), *Ex Officio Member*, National Academy of Engineering
Victor J. Dzau (NAM), *Ex Officio Member*, National Academy of Medicine
Marcia McNutt (NAS), *Ex Officio Member*, National Academy of Sciences

STAFF
Gail Cohen, Director
Rebecca Alcenius, Senior Project Assistant (through March 2020)
Meghan Ange-Stark, Associate Program Officer
Sophie Billinge, Senior Project Assistant
David Dierksheide, Program Officer
William Gaieck, Christine Mirzayan Science and Technology Policy Graduate Fellow (Winter 2020)
Frederic Lestina, Research Associate (through September 2020)
Clara Savage, Financial Officer

Preface

For more than 80 years, the United States federal laboratory system has been a bedrock of our national innovation system. In pursuit of a clear public mission, federal labs engage in complex, multidisciplinary R&D to address national scientific objectives that universities and firms are not equipped to undertake or that require significant investment of federal funds to respond to national emergencies. Renewed concern about the country's competitiveness and the potential loss of technological leadership to foreign firms has refocused policy makers' attention on maximizing returns on federal R&D investments, including by advancing the commercialization of digital products developed at the federal labs. Digital products developed by the federal labs include data, metadata, images, software, code, tools, databases, algorithms, and statistical models. These are all vital components of the national digital economic infrastructure, and they have assumed greater importance during the COVID-19 pandemic.

The committee's task was to determine ways to advance commercialization of these digital products. We analyzed issues surrounding technology transfer and ownership of digital products emerging from the labs—focusing on identifying barriers to commercialization and recommendations to overcome them. Notably, we tackled a long-standing distinction between federal labs that can own intellectual property and those precluded from so doing. We also reviewed the dynamic policy considerations that inform whether the public interest is best served by dedicating federally funded digital products to the public domain.

The committee's focus on potential benefits and limitations of open access models for dissemination led us to the conclusion that small, minority-owned, and woman-owned firms can be systemically excluded from accessing or exploiting government works freely available in the public domain because they lack the tools or resources to identify and exploit the vast number of works in the public domain. Moreover, we found that, at times, copyright ownership in federal software can improve opportunities for commercialization. Intellectual property ownership allows the federal labs to determine what avenues of commercialization will enhance returns to the public, including exerting control over downstream users to ensure the technology is made accessible to all members of the public. Overall, we found that improved coherence on intellectual property rights across federal labs can enhance equitable and robust access to federally funded digital products.

Another key finding in the report is that inadequate data on technology transfer limits the ability to undertake a comprehensive assessment of the antecedents and consequences of research commercialization by federal labs. There is a need for broader measures of technology transfer processes to reflect the full range of activities that lead up to commercialization. To better understand these processes, the committee also recognized the need for data on workplace/managerial practices relating to technology transfer, including individual and organizational factors that may inhibit or enhance lab researchers' ability to engage in technology transfer and commercialization. These factors include the role of pecuniary and nonpecuniary incentives, organizational justice (workplace fairness and equity), championing, leadership, work-life balance, diversity and inclusion, and organizational culture. Such data would help improve our understanding of the potential roadblocks faced by scientists at federal labs who wish to pursue commercialization of their research. It would also allow us to assess how "better performance" in technology transfer is achieved.

Based on its findings, the committee generated a series of recommendations that are discussed in the report. Two recommendations stand out to us as especially significant. The first is that Congress should consider allowing copyright on software developed by government-owned, government-operated federal laboratories on a prospective basis. The second is that there should be a significant expansion of data collection at the individual and organizational levels. We recognize that this will be an additional burden on the labs, and we hope that new tools and techniques of data collection will help reduce that burden. Collectively, our recommendations are directed at building a healthier, more effective, and resilient federal laboratory system that is better understood by policy makers and well equipped to perform the public mission that remains critical for America's scientific and technological progress and, ultimately, the welfare of her citizens.

ACKNOWLEDGMENTS

The committee benefitted considerably from presentations by speakers from academia, industry, and government. The invaluable leadership of National Academies' staff Gail Cohen, Study Director, and David Dierksheide, Program Officer, immeasurably improved the committee's deliberations and the final report. Their tireless efforts ensured that the committee captured the issues' complexity and addressed important details with diligence. We are also grateful to the dedication of other staff: Anita Eisenstadt, Frederic Lestina, and Clara Savage. Two subject matter experts who served as consultants to the committee—Professors Jerome Reichman and Jorge Contreras—made significant contributions that clarified essential dimensions of the committee's work, and consultants Robert Samors, Michael Baumer, and Honggi Lee skillfully guided the committee's framing of the overarching issues including technical analyses and data collection. We acknowledge all with deep gratitude.

Ruth Okediji   Donald S. Siegel

Acknowledgment of Reviewers

This Consensus Study Report was reviewed in draft form by individuals chosen for their diverse perspectives and technical expertise. The purpose of this independent review is to provide candid and critical comments that will assist the National Academies of Sciences, Engineering, and Medicine in making each published report as sound as possible and to ensure that it meets the institutional standards for quality, objectivity, evidence, and responsiveness to the study charge. The review comments and draft manuscript remain confidential to protect the integrity of the deliberative process.

We thank the following individuals for their review of this report: David Aspnes, North Carolina State University; Michael Carroll, American University; Gaétan de Rassenfosse, Swiss Federal Institute of Technology Lausanne; Brenda Dietrich, Cornell University; Dinesh Divakaran, Duke University; Robin Feldman, University of California, Hastings College of Law; Shubha Ghosh, Syracuse University; Shane Greenstein, Harvard University; Michael Harrison, University of California, San Francisco; Karen LeVert, Ag TechInventures; David Maier, Portland State University; Steven Porter, Stanford University (ret.); and Steve Ray, QUDT.

Although the reviewers listed above provided many constructive comments and suggestions, they were not asked to endorse the conclusions or recommendations of this report nor did they see the final draft before its release. The review of this report was overseen by Maryellen Giger, University of Chicago, and TJ Glauthier, TJG Energy Associates. They were responsible for making certain that an independent examination of this report was carried out in accordance with the standards of the National Academies and that all review comments were carefully considered. Responsibility for the final content rests entirely with the authoring committee and the National Academies.

Contents

SUMMARY   1

1 INTRODUCTION   15
Study Purpose and Scope, 16
Definitions of Technology Transfer, Commercialization, and
   Digital Products, 18
Organization of the Report, 19

2 THE U.S. FEDERAL LABORATORY SYSTEM   21
History and Evolution of the Federal Laboratories, 21
The Federal Laboratory Infrastructure, 23
Government-owned, Government-operated (GOGO) and
   Government-owned, Contractor-operated (GOCO)
   Laboratories, 23
Overview of the Research Activities of the Federal Laboratories, 24
Technology Transfer Legislation and Policy Relevant to Federal
   Laboratories, 25
Conclusion, 27

**3 DIGITAL PRODUCTS AND FEDERAL POLICY FOR
THE INNOVATION ECONOMY**   29
Digital Products and Innovation, 29
Intellectual Property Policy and Innovation in the Federal
   Laboratories, 30
The Economics of Digital Products, 35
Conclusion, 37
Findings and Recommendations, 37

**4 PATENTS, TRADE SECRETS, DIGITAL PRODUCTS,
AND FEDERAL LABORATORIES**   39
Patents, 39
Trade Secrets, 50

Intellectual Property Surrogates: Contractual and Technological
   Measures, 55
Findings and Recommendations, 56

5   COPYRIGHTS, DIGITAL PRODUCTS, AND FEDERAL LABORATORIES   59
Overview of Copyright in Digital Products, 59
The Government Works Copyright Exclusion, 61
Applying Copyright to Federally Created Software, 66
Limiting and Assessing Copyright and Exclusive Licensing
   of Software Developed by GOGO Federal Laboratories, 75
Advancing Coherence in Government Software Policy, 75
Findings and Recommendations, 76

6   TECHNOLOGY TRANSFER PATHWAYS FOR DIGITAL PRODUCTS   79
Technology Transfer Offices at the Federal Laboratories, 79
Technology Transfer and Dissemination Pathways, 81
Technology Transfer/Commercialization Ecosystem Enablers, 89
Incentives for Scientists and Engineers to Engage in Technology
   Transfer at Federal Laboratories, 89
Findings and Recommendations, 91

7   MEASURING THE COMMERCIALIZATION OF DIGITAL PRODUCTS FROM FEDERAL LABORATORIES   93
Overview and Assessment of Available Data, 94
Proposed New Metrics, 105
In Closing, 108
Findings and Recommendations, 108

REFERENCES   111

APPENDIXES

A   **Agendas**   125

B   **Biographies of Committee Members**   133

C   **Definitions of Digital Products**   139

D   **List of Federal Laboratories**   143

Summary

Federal laboratories play a unique role in the U.S. economy. Research and development (R&D) conducted at these labs has contributed to the advancement or improvement of such key general-purpose technologies as nuclear energy, computers, the Internet, genomics, satellite navigation, the Global Positioning System, artificial intelligence, and virtual reality. Federal labs also feature prominently in the nation's response to national and international emergencies, including the COVID-19 pandemic. A key feature of these labs is that they are heterogeneous with respect to their mission, operator (i.e., contractor vs. government operated), size, scale, and scope.

The U.S. government made major investments in federal labs during World War II, most notably to support the Manhattan Project, as well as in the postwar period. For many years, federal labs stood alongside a range of well-established corporate labs that participated in all stages of R&D in the United States. In the late 1970s, however, increased global competition led Congress to enact legislation designed to spur the commercialization of research at universities and federal labs. Recently, renewed concern about the potential loss of technological leadership to foreign competitors has refocused attention on federal laboratory innovation and stimulated interest in determining how to maximize returns on federal investments in R&D, including by advancing commercialization of R&D performed at federal labs.

Recent administrations have articulated the goal of improving the transfer of federally funded technologies, including technologies created by the federal government, through Lab-to-Market initiatives. The National Institute of Standards and Technology (NIST) and other federal agencies, with the support of the Office of Science and Technology Policy (OSTP) and the Office of Management and Budget (OMB), have determined that developing new strategies for improving the assessment and commercialization of digital products is a priority area for the Lab-to-Market Cross-Agency Priority (CAP) goal.

STUDY PURPOSE AND SCOPE

Innovation has enabled capabilities in data collection, computation, simulation, and analysis unheard of even a decade ago, yet the technology transfer and commercialization of digital products are not well understood. Digital output from federal laboratories includes data, metadata, images, software, code, tools, databases, algorithms, and statistical models. Importantly, these digital products are nonrivalrous, meaning that unlike physical products, they can be copied at little or no cost and used by many without limit or additional cost.

In this context, the National Academies of Sciences, Engineering, and Medicine convened an ad hoc committee of experts to consider issues surrounding the use and ownership of government digital products. The committee examined the current state of commercialization of digital products developed at the federal labs and, to a limited extent, by extramural awardees, to help identify barriers to commercialization and technology transfer, taking into account differences between government-owned, contractor-operated (GOCO) and government-owned, government-operated (GOGO) federal labs. In this report, the committee presents the findings of its study and offers recommendations for improving the commercialization of digital products generated by federal labs. To reach its findings and formulate its recommendations, the committee reviewed the salient literature, and over the course of the study convened a series of public meetings and heard from a broad range of expert speakers, including federal agency technology transfer experts, representatives from industry, and researchers studying the challenges and potential of commercializing digital products from federal labs.

KEY FINDINGS

Through its analysis of and deliberations on the information gathered from the above sources, the committee developed 14 findings. All of these findings address notable aspects of technology transfer and commercialization for digital products from federal laboratories, but 5 of the 14 stood out to the committee as especially important. These 5 key findings are discussed below: 3 of the findings relate to trade-offs between open and exclusive access to data and software; 1 finding relates to the lack of copyright available to GOGO labs; and 1 finding relates to available metrics for assessing transfers of digital technologies created within the labs. All 14 findings are included in Box S-1 at the end of this summary.

Three overarching findings reflect the committee's conviction that although much of what is produced by the federal labs should be openly and freely available without any control exercised by the government, the public interest may in some cases best be served by the government's exercise of proprietary interests to facilitate opportunities for commercialization. Thus, the committee acknowledges the benefits of making government data freely available to facilitate commercialization of products stemming from the use of these data, consistent with existing federal law and policies around government-produced information. Similarly, the committee concluded that federally produced digital products, such as software, should be freely available in most instances. At the same time, however, the committee recognized that there may be cases in which the granting of exclusive rights to a firm is necessary to promote additional investment in innovation to facilitate commercialization of products emanating from federal labs. Furthermore, small, minority-owned, and woman-owned firms can be systemically excluded from accessing or exploiting government works freely available in the public domain because they lack the tools or resources to identify and exploit the vast number of works dedicated to the public.

Federal labs are neither well suited nor chartered to directly commercialize their work products. Therefore, technology transfer from federal labs to the marketplace is possible only through participation of the private sector, often through formal or informal partnerships, highlighting the need for economic incentives to make such partnerships feasible. Most digital products created in federal labs may not be directly usable off the shelf and require substantial additional investments. In such cases, it may be that only an exclusive license would provide returns sufficient to incentivize a private firm to invest in a product's further development. Acting in the public interest will require balancing a variety of factors to determine when government stewardship is best accomplished by allowing exclusive use by a firm, by the adoption of open-access licensing, or by dedication to the public domain (with or without a license) to advance scientific progress and innovation.

> *Finding 3-1: Making government data freely and openly available maximizes the use, reuse, and therefore the value of these data for commercial and noncommercial entities.*
>
> *Finding 3-2: Federally produced digital products often yield large societal benefits when widely distributed, although federal laboratories may need to restrict access to those products when significant and costly follow-on development by firms is needed to commercialize them.*
>
> *Finding 3-3: While placing digital products in the public domain may reduce obstacles to their use, reliance on the public domain alone will not enable the participation of small firms, minority-owned firms, woman-owned firms, and members of society that lack the market networks, resources, and tools to discover and exploit what is available in the public domain.*

Issues surrounding the government's ability to assert intellectual property rights in digital products, most notably software, are a key consideration in advancing their commercialization. Put differently, the ability of federal labs to control disposition of their digital products has a significant impact on the range of dissemination pathways available to them. For example, without copyright, GOGO labs cannot make the same choices available to GOCO labs regarding the disposition of their software. Instead, GOGO labs may rely on trade secrets or intellectual property surrogates to exert downstream controls over the use of government-created software, which may have a chilling effect on innovation more broadly.

The committee's fourth key finding stems from the heterogeneity of the federal labs, especially with regard to operational differences. Reflecting these differences, the application of intellectual property law to the federal labs has been inconsistent over the years, and lacks a single set of guiding principles. Section 105 of the Copyright Act excludes GOGO labs from being able to claim copyright in their digital products, thus limiting the channels available to them for disseminating and commercializing those products relative to GOCO labs, which are allowed to assert copyright in their digital products. This situation likely has arisen from a combination of historical accident, uncoordinated decision making across a range of agencies and legal domains, and the accumulation of special-purpose exceptions (some directed by Congress) that have persisted over the years. As a result, GOGO labs have developed different mechanisms for dealing with their inability to claim copyright for government works, limitations that in some cases may not enhance the public interest or be consistent with prevailing legal doctrines.

> ***Finding 5-2: The inability of government-owned, government-operated laboratories to assert copyright in federally developed software creates incentives for those labs to circumvent existing rules in order to facilitate technology transfer and commercialization.***

Finally, the committee recognizes that currently available data permit only a limited understanding of the commercialization of digital products generated by federal labs. Data on commercialized products, processes, and services—including digital products—produced from knowledge or inventions created in federal labs are extremely limited, and there are currently no metrics that can fully capture the longer-term economic impact of what the labs produce, particularly over the long run. Researchers and policy makers are generally confined to considering inputs into invention (e.g., R&D spending and knowledge transfer via publications), evidence for selected inventions (patents), and limited metrics for only two of the pathways (i.e., licenses and cooperative agreements) by which knowledge and technology are transferred out of the labs.

The limited data on technology transfer do not sufficiently advance understanding of the commercialization of digital products from federal labs. More specifically, the technology transfer data that are available (for example, from cooperative research partnerships, licenses, and patents) are not disaggregated by type of underlying invention (such as whether a patent or license relates to software or another digital invention) or by individual lab. Most of the data is reported at the agency level, which is too high a level of aggregation to aid in understanding the commercialization process. The information that is collected also reflects formal mechanisms of traditional technology transfer, such as licenses and royalties, rather than informal mechanisms or newer routes of technology transfer used especially for digital products, such as the number of software or data downloads, conference presentations, or papers. Although the number of licenses is reported, that information does not include how many of the licenses are open-source software (OSS) versus exclusive or partially exclusive licenses. Moreover, no information is collected from individual scientists at the federal labs that could be used to determine what incentives and what barriers they face in transferring their technology out of the lab. Finally, there are no measures of actual commercialization on the part of firms—that is, market introduction of data, software, or other digital products originating from the labs.

> *Finding 7-1: Both existing metrics on federal laboratory activities that may result in the commercialization of digital products and the reporting of these metrics are inadequate. Thus, they do not allow for a comprehensive assessment of the commercialization of either digital products arising from research at federal labs or the federally developed inputs into that research, including their broader impact on the economy.*

KEY RECOMMENDATIONS

From its full set of 19 recommendations, the committee identified 8 key recommendations that warrant highlighting. These 8 recommendations fall into three categories: (1) the need for policy coherence in ownership of intellectual property rights related to digital products across all federal laboratories; (2) the need for uniform public interest requirements for exclusive licensing of digital products created in federal labs; and (3) the need for additional data collection and reporting on technology transfer and commercialization of digital products created at federal labs. The full set of 19 recommendations is presented in Box S-2 at the end of this summary.

The first key recommendation stems from the need for uniformity around intellectual property rights across federal labs, as noted in the discussion of Finding 5-2. Unlike GOCO labs, GOGO labs are not permitted to hold copyright in federally developed software, and the committee found evidence that this restriction may inhibit the ability of GOGO labs to issue both exclusive licenses, when needed, and OSS licenses, relative to GOCO labs, which have a broader range of tools at their disposal for commercializing their research outputs. Efforts by some GOGO labs to circumvent the lack of copyright protection for software through contractual, trade secret, or other mechanisms may result in suboptimal commercial and public interest outcomes. Thus, the committee recommends that

Congress consider allowing GOGO labs to hold copyright in their federally developed digital products.

> **Recommendation 5-1: Congress should consider amending Section 105(a) of the Copyright Act to allow copyright on software developed by government-owned, government-operated federal laboratories on a prospective basis, subject to a number of limitations, as described in Recommendation 5-2. The amendment should also require that each agency collect appropriate data to determine the impact of such a change.**

Three of the committee's key recommendations fall into the category of gaps in the public interest requirement in Section 209 of the Bayh-Dole Act. Section 209 allows agencies to grant exclusive licenses for government-produced inventions only if such licenses are necessary to encourage private-sector investment needed for commercialization or otherwise to promote an invention's use by the public. No statutory public interest requirements are imposed on GOCO labs, although some federal agencies have issued directives to these labs following the concepts laid out in Section 209. Moreover, these requirements apply only to licenses for patented inventions and not copyright licenses. The committee believes that exclusive licensing by federal labs should be allowed only when it meets the public interest requirements laid out in Section 209, regardless of the type of federal lab or the type of intellectual property right associated with the digital product. This public interest requirement will ensure the broadest reach of publicly funded and government-created technologies and enable healthy competition among firms and other actors to receive and benefit from the public's investment. With respect to software, because software development cycles are relatively short, agencies should limit the period of time allowed for exclusive licenses.

> **Recommendation 4-3: Congress should consider imposing public interest licensing requirements on government-owned, contractor-operated laboratory contractors that are comparable to those imposed on their government-owned, government-operated counterparts under Section 209 of the Bayh-Dole Act.**
>
> **Recommendation 5-2: Any exclusive software copyright license issued by a government-owned, government-operated federal laboratory should be subject to the following limitations:**
>
> - **Consideration of the costs and benefits of granting exclusive versus nonexclusive licenses or contributing**

SUMMARY

the relevant work to the public domain, including what is needed to bring the software to practical application or to promote its utilization for the public benefit.
- A limit of 10 years' duration or a shorter period of time sufficient to commercialize the relevant software. A waiver of this time limit could be considered if licensees provided sufficient justification.
- Announcement in the *Federal Register* of the proposed grant of exclusive rights, together with the justification for it, and consideration of public comments made in response to that announcement.

In addition, the committee notes that parties harmed by violations of Section 209 public interest requirements have little legal recourse, and recommends that such parties be given stronger means of recourse.

Recommendation 4-2: Congress should consider enacting mechanisms that provide greater legal force to public interest licensing requirements. For example, the violation of such requirements could be recognized as an affirmative defense to a claim of infringement by an exclusive licensee of a federal patent or give rise to a private cause of action for such violation.

Finally, the committee recognizes the need for a substantial amount of additional data on technology transfer and commercialization of digital products from federal labs, while also recognizing the substantial costs associated with collecting these data. Accordingly, the committee recommends that new data be collected at the individual, lab, firm, and user levels, and that federal agencies allocate sufficient resources for these efforts. Especially important is collecting information about the outcomes of cooperative agreements between labs and external partners (firms, universities, and other nonprofit organizations). Cooperative ventures, and cooperative research and development agreements (CRADAs) in particular, are widely recognized as important mechanisms for technology transfer from federal labs to industry.

Implementation of the committee's recommendations regarding new data collection and reporting would provide needed information on the use and dissemination of knowledge, data, and software emanating from the labs. The committee also recognizes the need for data on workplace/organizational practices relating to technology transfer, including individual and organizational factors that may inhibit or enhance the ability of lab researchers to engage in technology transfer and commercialization activities. These factors include pecuniary and nonpecuniary incentives, organizational justice (workplace fairness and equity), championing, leadership, work–life balance, and organizational culture. These data at the individual and organizational levels would help improve understanding of the potential roadblocks faced by scientists at federal labs who wish to pursue commercialization of their research. To reduce the associated cost and time burden, the government could use public and commercially available data and new research tools, whenever possible, to supplement or replace efforts required for the proposed surveys and reduce costs. Burdensome requirements for additional data collection and failure to take advantage of automated data collection could provide disincentives to technology transfer and knowledge dissemination.

> **Recommendation 7-1:** The Interagency Working Group on Technology Transfer and the National Science Foundation should coordinate on the collection of a more comprehensive set of metrics on both the inputs and outputs of those federal laboratory activities that may result in commercialization of digital products. These metrics should be reported in the annual report to Congress from the National Institute of Standards and Technology. These metrics should include, but not be limited to, participation in public conferences or meetings, technology transfer budgets, number of employees in the technology transfer office of each lab, research and development (R&D) budgets, the composition of R&D (e.g., percentage of effort devoted to basic research, applied research, and development), software downloads, software licenses, data downloads, cooperative arrangements, software licensing royalties, invention disclosures, patents, and copyrights. This information should be tracked annually and reported publicly at the individual lab level except where national security might be compromised.
>
> **Recommendation 7-2:** The National Institute of Standards and Technology or the Office of Management and Budget should direct federal agencies to provide a more comprehensive accounting of the activities of and results produced by all cooperative research and development agreements and all other cooperative arrangements between the federal laboratories and the private sector, including accounting of failures.
>
> **Recommendation 7-3:** The National Science Foundation's National Center for Science and Engineering Statistics (NCSES) should develop survey questions for firms, in accordance with Paperwork Reduction Act requirements, regarding the data, software, digital content, knowledge, and inventions originating from the federal laboratories that have contributed to firms' commercialization of new products,

processes, and services. Firms should also report on the patents, processes, and products to which the outputs of the federal labs have contributed. These survey questions should encompass firms' cooperative activities with the labs and the usability of datasets and software released by the labs. These questions could be included in NCSES's Annual Business Survey or in a separate survey should NCSES conclude that this would be a more effective means of data collection.

Recommendation 6-2: An appropriate federal agency should conduct a study of the potential impact of different incentive and organizational factors on the motivation of federal laboratory researchers to engage in technology transfer and commercialization and the success of such efforts. Federal labs should use the results of this study when considering changes to their incentive structure and organizational practices.

FINAL THOUGHTS

The approaches to technology transfer of the different federal laboratories show considerable variation. The labs have different missions and norms, and research and technology development efforts are often not coordinated across labs, even those within the same federal agency. The labs also differ in size, scale, and scope. Moreover, different types of digital products are not always amenable to the same dissemination and commercialization pathways. To serve the public interest, federal labs—regardless of whether they are GOGO or GOCO labs—should have access to all tools available for advancing innovation and commercializing federally funded research.

In accordance with their missions, federal labs are engaged in the creation of knowledge and the generation of inventions. Much of this activity, however, is not reflected in the annual technology transfer report. Rather, that report focuses on formal activities (patents, licenses, and CRADAs) that in most cases involve a transfer of money. No data are collected on software or data that are made freely available through open-source portals. The only information collected on intellectual property created by the labs relates to patents and their licensing. Nor is any information collected on copyright, even for GOCO labs, which are able to claim copyright for software and other works of authorship. Better tracking of these activities would not be without cost. Therefore, additional resources are needed to understand technology transfer and other activities that affect the commercialization of a lab's R&D outputs, including those related to digital products. Federal labs must be given sufficient resources to collect this information as well as to properly maintain, store, and curate their data and software collections without impinging on their core missions or creating perverse incentives to restrict access in order to generate needed revenue.

> **BOX S-1**
> **Complete List of Findings**
>
> *Finding 3-1*: Making government data freely and openly available maximizes the use, reuse, and therefore the value of these data for commercial and noncommercial entities.
>
> *Finding 3-2*: Federally produced digital products often yield large societal benefits when widely distributed, although federal laboratories may need to restrict access to those products when significant and costly follow-on development by firms is needed to commercialize them.
>
> *Finding 3-3*: While placing digital products in the public domain may reduce obstacles to their use, reliance on the public domain alone will not enable the participation of small firms, minority-owned firms, woman-owned firms, and members of society that lack the market networks, resources, and tools to discover and exploit what is available in the public domain.
>
> *Finding 4-1*: Given documented cases in which federal laboratories have licensed software patents to patent assertion entities, it appears that federal labs do not always adhere to the requirements in Section 209 of the Bayh-Dole Act, which include allowing licensing only if such action is necessary to achieve practical application. However, evidence of how common such breaches are is limited. At the same time, there appears to be no effective remedy for violation of the Section 209 requirements on the part of federal agencies.
>
> *Finding 4-2*: Exclusive software licenses are less valuable to the private sector if the software and source code are accessible via the Freedom of Information Act (FOIA). Using trade secrets to protect federal software, including source code, limits its accessibility to the public under FOIA.
>
> *Finding 4-3*: Differences among federal agencies with respect to the trade secret exemption from the Freedom of Information Act appear to have no clear policy rationale.
>
> *Finding 4-4*: Over the years, federal laboratories have taken advantage of a number of mechanisms—including nondisclosure agreements, license agreements, restrictions on redisclosure of information, and other types of controls—to extend their control over federal digital products, even in the absence of recognized intellectual property protection.
>
> *Finding 5-1*: With some exceptions, the Copyright Act prohibits copyright in federally created works, and the federal government maintains a general policy of making such works accessible in a manner consistent with the public interest.
>
> *Finding 5-2*: The inability of government-owned, government-operated laboratories to assert copyright in federally developed software creates incentives for those labs to circumvent existing rules in order to facilitate technology transfer and commercialization.

Finding 5-3: The statutory authorization of standard reference data (SRD) copyright has little legal justification. Moreover, there appears to be no economic rationale for retaining copyright in SRD because the National Institute of Standards and Technology, the current custodian and developer of SRD, makes 80 percent of SRD available free of charge without copyright and earns an insignificant amount from the remaining SRD.

Finding 5-4: Assertion of foreign copyright by federal agencies in works for which they lack U.S. copyright is inconsistent with the Berne Convention, to which the United States acceded in 1989, as well as prevailing U.S. conflict-of-laws principles.

Finding 6-1: Although the approaches taken by federal laboratories to the dissemination and commercialization of digital publications and data are generally consistent, the approaches taken with respect to software vary across labs.

Finding 6-2: Studies of individual and organizational factors in university technology transfer have yielded insights on the importance of incentives (both financial and nonfinancial), championing, and other managerial practices in stimulating technology commercialization and entrepreneurship, but there have been few such studies of managerial practices in the federal laboratory context.

Finding 7-1: Both existing metrics on federal laboratory activities that may result in the commercialization of digital products and the reporting of these metrics are inadequate. Thus, they do not allow for a comprehensive assessment of the commercialization of either digital products arising from research at federal labs or the federally developed inputs into that research, including their broader impact on the economy.

BOX S-2
Complete List of Recommendations

Recommendation 3-1: Federal laboratory directors should ensure that data and associated metadata produced by their labs are freely and openly available for use by individuals, researchers, and firms to the fullest extent possible under existing statutes and policies.

Recommendation 3-2: When additional substantial investment by the private sector is necessary to commercialize a digital innovation and the ultimate product is readily imitable, a federal laboratory director should allow exclusive access to that innovation to incentivize such investment.

Recommendation 3-3: Federal laboratory directors should consider ways to identify and support small, minority-owned, and woman-owned firms and members of society that may not be in a position to identify freely available digital goods, may not know how to interface with the federal labs on such matters, and/or may not understand how the use of these digital products may be relevant to their interests. Federal lab directors should proactively address such disparities in access.

Recommendation 4-1: The Government Accountability Office or another appropriate, independent government entity should regularly, but not less than biennially, conduct a comprehensive assessment of the federal laboratories' compliance with public interest requirements in Section 209 of the Bayh-Dole Act related to issuance of exclusive patent licenses.

Recommendation 4-2: Congress should consider enacting mechanisms that provide greater legal force to public interest licensing requirements. For example, the violation of such requirements could be recognized as an affirmative defense to a claim of infringement by an exclusive licensee of a federal patent or give rise to a private cause of action for such violation.

Recommendation 4-3: Congress should consider imposing public interest licensing requirements on government-owned, contractor-operated laboratory contractors that are comparable to those imposed on their government-owned, government-operated counterparts under Section 209 of the Bayh-Dole Act.

Recommendation 4-4: Congress should consider rescinding the Section 801 authority provided by the 2008 National Defense Authorization Act that allows agencies to assert trade secrets even for unclassified information with no national security implication.

Recommendation 5-1: Congress should consider amending Section 105(a) of the Copyright Act to allow copyright on software developed by government-owned, government-operated federal laboratories on a prospective basis, subject to a number of limitations, as described in Recommendation 5-2. The amendment should also require that each agency collect appropriate data to determine the impact of such a change.

Recommendation 5-2: Any exclusive software copyright license issued by a government-owned, government-operated federal laboratory should be subject to the following limitations:

- Consideration of the costs and benefits of granting exclusive versus nonexclusive licenses or contributing the relevant work to the public domain, including what is needed to bring the software to practical application or to promote its utilization for the public benefit.
- A limit of 10 years' duration or a shorter period of time sufficient to commercialize the relevant software. A waiver of this time limit could be considered if licensees provided sufficient justification.
- Announcement in the *Federal Register* of the proposed grant of exclusive rights, together with the justification for it, and consideration of public comments made in response to that announcement.

Recommendation 5-3: If Congress does create an exception to Section 105(a) of the Copyright Act for software developed by government-owned, government-operated laboratories, the National Institute of Standards and Technology should commission a study to determine whether and how changing the law has affected the use, dissemination, and commercialization of federally developed software.

Recommendation 5-4: If Congress does not amend Section 105(a) of the Copyright Act to allow government-owned, government-operated laboratories to hold copyright in federally created software, the director of the National Institute of Standards and Technology should develop a uniform federal software contribution agreement that does not depend on copyright, to be made available for use by all federal labs on a voluntary basis.

Recommendation 5-5: Congress should consider repealing the recognition of copyright in standard reference data (SRD) under the SRD Act.

Recommendation 5-6: The Department of Justice's Office of Legal Counsel should issue an advisory opinion to all federal agencies clarifying that in general, foreign copyright is presumed to be unavailable with respect to works covered by the government works exclusion under Section 105(a) of the Copyright Act.

Recommendation 6-1: The Federal Interagency Working Group on Technology Transfer should develop a set of written best practices for federal laboratories to use in determining dissemination pathways for lab-developed software.

Recommendation 6-2: An appropriate federal agency should conduct a study of the potential impact of different incentive and organizational factors on the motivation of federal laboratory researchers to engage in technology transfer and commercialization and the success of such efforts. Federal labs should use the results of this study when considering changes to their incentive structure and organizational practices.

(Continued)

BOX S-2
Continued

Recommendation 7-1: The Interagency Working Group on Technology Transfer and the National Science Foundation should coordinate on the collection of a more comprehensive set of metrics on both the inputs and outputs of those federal laboratory activities that may result in commercialization of digital products. These metrics should be reported in the annual report to Congress from the National Institute of Standards and Technology. These metrics should include, but not be limited to, participation in public conferences or meetings, technology transfer budgets, number of employees in the technology transfer office of each lab, research and development (R&D) budgets, the composition of R&D (e.g., percentage of effort devoted to basic research, applied research, and development), software downloads, software licenses, data downloads, cooperative arrangements, software licensing royalties, invention disclosures, patents, and copyrights. This information should be tracked annually and reported publicly at the individual lab level except where national security might be compromised.

Recommendation 7-2: The National Institute of Standards and Technology or the Office of Management and Budget should direct federal agencies to provide a more comprehensive accounting of the activities of and results produced by all cooperative research and development agreements and all other cooperative arrangements between the federal laboratories and the private sector, including accounting of failures.

Recommendation 7-3: The National Science Foundation's National Center for Science and Engineering Statistics (NCSES) should develop survey questions for firms, in accordance with Paperwork Reduction Act requirements, regarding the data, software, digital content, knowledge, and inventions originating from the federal laboratories that have contributed to firms' commercialization of new products, processes, and services. Firms should also report on the patents, processes, and products to which the outputs of the federal labs have contributed. These survey questions should encompass firms' cooperative activities with the labs and the usability of datasets and software released by the labs. These questions could be included in NCSES's Annual Business Survey or in a separate survey should NCSES conclude that this would be a more effective means of data collection.

Recommendation 7-4: Federal agencies should dedicate sufficient resources to measurement such that analysts and policy makers will have the information needed to develop recommendations regarding the federal laboratories' technology transfer and other activities that impact the commercialization of the labs' research and development outputs, including those related to digital products. To this end, the National Science Foundation should standardize the collection and reporting of the current data elements and those proposed by the committee. The Office of Management and Budget and Congress should support both the efforts of the National Center for Science and Engineering Statistics to develop and conduct these surveys and the efforts of the labs to meet these data collection requirements.

1

Introduction

Federal laboratories play a unique role in the U.S. economy. They solve important problems in fundamental science, and they "design, build, and operate distinctive scientific instrumentation and facilities" that serve a variety of scientists and engineers from the government, academia, and industry (NIST, 2019a, p. 57). Although often referred to by the umbrella term "federal laboratories," these entities are actually a heterogeneous group of organizations with differences in their types of operators; their missions; and their size, scale, and geography. Thus a federal laboratory is defined as "any laboratory, any federally funded research and development center (FFRDC), or any center that is owned, leased, or otherwise used by a Federal agency and funded by the Federal Government, whether operated by the Government or by a contractor" (15 U.S.C. § 3703). Operational structures include government-owned, government-operated (GOGO) and government-owned, contractor-operated (GOCO). Of the billions of dollars the federal government invests annually in research and development (R&D) (more than $115 billion in fiscal year 2016), more than one-third is invested in federal labs (NIST, 2019a).

The role of the federal labs has changed over time. Prior to World War II, "most of the federal funds for R&D supported mission-oriented research in agriculture, national defense, and natural resources carried out by government employees in small government laboratories and experimental stations" (IOM et al., 1995, p. 41). Responding to the increased need for R&D in wartime, the federal government made major investments in research labs and established new administrative mechanisms to manage R&D programs. In the early 1980s, increased competition from other countries, especially for new products based on advanced technological capabilities, together with a decline in corporate labs that participated in all stages of the R&D process, led Congress to pass legislation designed to spur the commercialization of industrially related R&D at universities and federal labs (IOM et al., 1995).

Recent renewed concern about the potential loss of U.S. technological leadership to emerging foreign competitors has refocused attention on federal lab innovation and stimulated greater attention to optimizing returns on federal investments. Indeed, improving the transfer of federally funded technologies through Lab-to-Market initiatives has been a priority of recent administrations. The Lab-to-Market Cross Agency Priority (CAP) goal aimed to "improve the transfer of technology from federally funded research and development to the private sector to promote U.S. economic growth and national security" (Executive Office of the President, 2018, p. 47).

The National Institute of Standards and Technology (NIST) has a leading role in coordinating technology transfer efforts across the federal government. The agency co-chairs the National Science and Technology Council's Lab-to-Market subcommittee and, in conjunction with the Department of Energy and the White House Office of Science and Technology Policy (OSTP), oversees the subcommittee's activities and the implementation of the Lab-to-Market CAP goal. NIST and other federal agencies, with the support of OSTP and the Office of Management and Budget (OMB), have determined that developing new strategies for improving the assessment and commercialization of digital products is a priority area for the Lab-to-Market CAP goal. This report examines a variety of legal and policy tools available to federal labs for disseminating and commercializing their digital products and related knowledge.

STUDY PURPOSE AND SCOPE

The purpose of this study of the National Academies of Sciences, Engineering, and Medicine was to identify and prioritize opportunities for adding economic value to U.S. industry, and thereby growing the U.S. economy and encouraging the development of products and services for the public's benefit, through enhanced utilization of intellectual property associated with digital products created at federal laboratories. To carry out this study, the National Academies convened an ad hoc committee under the auspices of the Board on Science, Technology, and Economic Policy (STEP), Policy and Global Affairs. The committee was charged to (1) examine commercialization of digital products resulting from federally funded R&D at the federal labs, as well as extramural awardees; (2) consider issues concerning the ownership, use, and repurposing of data and the effect of data use restrictions on the use and analysis of multiple datasets from different sources; (3) examine the current state of and barriers to commercialization of digital products; (4) evaluate approaches that GOCO and GOGO federal labs can use to incentivize their researchers and the private sector to commercialize digital products; (5) review open-source versus protected proprietary control of digital products and the factors that lead to determining a pathway for commercialization; and (6) offer recommendations for improvements, especially with regard to increasing the commercialization and use of these digital products in the private sector. The formal statement of task for this study is presented in Box 1-1.

In addition to reviewing the salient literature and holding closed-session discussions, the committee convened a series of public meetings and heard from a broad range of experts over the course of the study to ensure that the perspectives of practitioners in the public and private sectors and other experts would be taken into account. Experts addressing the committee ranged from agency management office representatives, to a broad range of representatives from federal labs, to individuals from industry and other private entities seeking to utilize federal lab outputs, to researchers studying the challenges and potential of commercializing digital products from federal labs. The evidence thus gathered served as the basis for the findings and recommendations presented in this report.

A central consideration in this report is the degree to which exclusive access is sometimes necessary for firms to commercialize digital products from federal labs, with the benefits of that commercialization accruing to the American economy in a manner consistent with the public interest. As described in detail in Chapter 3, in some cases, commercializing products from federal labs requires

---

BOX 1-1
Statement of Task for This Study

An ad hoc committee under the auspices of the Board on Science, Technology, and Economic Policy (STEP) will identify and prioritize opportunities to add economic value to U.S. industry through enhanced utilization of intellectual property around digital products created at federal laboratories. Specifically, the committee will

(1) examine commercialization of digital products from federally funded R&D at laboratories and extramural awardees;
(2) consider issues in the ownership, use, and repurposing of data, and the effect of data use restrictions on the use and analysis of multiple data sets from different sources;
(3) examine the current state of commercialization of digital products, including barriers to commercialization of digital products;
(4) evaluate approaches for government-owned, contractor-operator (GOCO) and government-owned, government-operated (GOGO) federal labs to incentivize their researchers and the private sector to commercialize digital products;
(5) review open source versus protected proprietary control of digital products and the factors that lead to making a determination of a selected pathway for commercialization; and
(6) offer recommendations for improvements regarding these digital products, especially with regard to increasing commercialization and use of these digital products in the private sector.

The committee will convene one public workshop and will issue a consensus report at the conclusion of the study.

substantial additional investment. Open access to these products may therefore, in these cases, discourage commercialization if firms are unwilling to make these additional investments in an environment in which other firms, both in the United States and abroad, have equal access to the output from the labs. This issue is expected to be particularly acute with respect to *digital* products—the subject of this report—which are unique in that they have nearly zero costs of reproduction, and multiple users can share them at no additional cost. In addition, as also described in the chapters that follow, there are important public welfare considerations that argue for exclusivity in certain instances.

DEFINITIONS OF TECHNOLOGY TRANSFER, COMMERCIALIZATION, AND DIGITAL PRODUCTS

As a baseline for its analysis, the committee adopted a set of definitions reflecting a broad view of digital products, technology transfer, and commercialization. For purposes of this report, "digital products" are defined as follows:

> Digital products are tangible and intangible representations of ideas, measurements, methods, or works, including in electronic formats. The two primary types of digital products addressed by this study are *data* and *software*. Detailed definitions of the different types of digital products are contained in Appendix C.

The term "technology transfer" is defined as follows:

> Technology transfer is the process, employing a broad range of mechanisms, by which knowledge, know-how, capabilities, or facilities at federal laboratories are used to meet public and private needs. Public and private needs include the advancement of science and technology, military readiness, improving and extending the quality of life, and economic and societal benefits.

Finally, "commercialization" of digital products is defined as follows:

> Commercialization is the process by which research findings, inventions, and data are transitioned to productive applications that contribute to economic and societal benefits. Commercialization occurs through a variety of mechanisms, including, but not limited to, cooperative ventures, sales, licensing, and the public release of data and scientific information via publications, reports, and presentations.

ORGANIZATION OF THE REPORT

The remainder of this report reviews the available evidence relevant to the purpose of this study (as described above) and presents the committee's findings and recommendations based on its analysis of that evidence. Chapter 2 describes the history and evolution of the federal laboratories; their involvement in science and innovation, including variations in their research mandates; and their organizational and administrative structures. Chapter 3 provides brief background on the economics of digital products, explaining why baseline rules and norms for regulating these products differ in important ways from those applied to technologies of the industrial era. Chapter 4 explores the federal patent and trade secrets regimes available to and utilized by the federal labs across a spectrum of digital products, including the implications of those regimes that bear on the subject of this study. Chapter 5 examines the copyright regime and its applicability to digital products, primarily software, produced by federal labs. Chapter 6 examines the various pathways for technology transfer of digital products from federal labs and the role of individual, organizational, and institutional factors in those pathways. Chapter 7 considers the effectiveness of methods for measuring the impact of technology transfer and of the commercialization of digital products. Following a compilation of references cited in the report, Appendix A includes agendas for the meetings held by the committee; Appendix B provides biographical information on the committee members; Appendix C contains definitions of digital products generated by the federal labs; and Appendix D presents a detailed listing of the federal labs, including the membership of the Federal Laboratory Consortium and the FFRDCs.

2

The U.S. Federal Laboratory System

This chapter briefly summarizes the historical, statutory, and organizational framework of the contemporary U.S. federal laboratory system. It highlights those aspects of the statutory and organizational framework most relevant to technology transfer and commercialization in the context of digital products.

HISTORY AND EVOLUTION OF THE FEDERAL LABORATORIES

As noted in Chapter 1, a federal laboratory is defined as "any laboratory, any federally funded research and development center (FFRDC), or any center that is owned, leased, or otherwise used by a Federal agency and funded by the Federal Government, whether operated by the Government or by a contractor" (15 U.S.C. § 3703). As public institutions, the federal labs are mission driven and engaged mainly in basic, foundational research that many private firms are unlikely to undertake. Some have played national security roles.

Beginning with the establishment of the Smithsonian Institution in 1846, the modern federal laboratory complex developed steadily over the 19th and 20th centuries and contributed to advances in science and technology that defined the nation during that period. Less than two decades later, in 1862, the Department of Agriculture was created, ushering in the Agricultural Research Service and the Public Health Service (now the National Institutes of Health) shortly thereafter in 1887. Each of these well-known federal institutions manages labs that have had significant impacts on the everyday lives of the American public. Several labs opened later under the auspices of the War Department (and later were transferred to what became the Department of Energy [DOE]). These labs, which included Ames, Argonne, Lawrence Berkeley (Radiation Lab), Los Alamos, Oak Ridge, and Pacific Northwest (Hanford Laboratory), were run by contractors and were critical to the World War II Manhattan Project, splitting uranium atoms and developing the atomic bomb.

Federal labs have long played a key role in technology development. In the field of computing, technological breakthroughs enabled by the focus of the federal labs on basic research have led to such important developments as the first electronic digital computer, ENIAC, developed by the Ordnance Ballistic Research Laboratory of the U.S. Army in collaboration with the University of Pennsylvania (Price and Siegel, 2019). The invention of touchscreen technology that can be manipulated with a finger or stylus was based on research conducted at Oak Ridge National Laboratory (Price and Siegel, 2019). The National Aeronautics and Space Administration's (NASA's) Ames Research Center, along with the Defense Advanced Research Projects Agency (DARPA), the Air Force Institute of Technology, the National Science Foundation, and National Institutes of Health (NIH), provided extensive funding for the development of virtual reality (VR) technology for uses ranging from gaming and entertainment, to medicine, to aerospace, to military applications (Price and Siegel, 2019). The Global Positioning System (GPS) signal that powers navigation applications around the world was originally developed by the U.S. Navy and continues to be maintained by the Department of Defense (DOD) (O'Connor et al., 2019). And the scientific fields of genomics and related "omics" (e.g., proteomics, transcriptomics, metabolomics, pharmacogenomics), all of which run on data, owe their existence to the foundational work of federal agencies conducted before, during, and after the Human Genome Project (HGP) (Contreras and Knoppers, 2018). The U.S. component of the HGP was led by NIH and the DOE, which together provided $3.8 billion in funding over the project's 15-year duration.[1] The HGP, which published the first draft of the human genomic sequence in 2001, was heralded as one of the most important scientific projects of all time (Tripp and Grueber, 2013).

The federal labs also feature prominently in the nation's emergency response plans of action for national and international emergencies, which have entailed securing at-risk nuclear materials in the former Soviet Union, assisting Japan in its response to the Fukushima nuclear reactor accident, responding to the international Ebola outbreak, and addressing oil and natural gas leaks in the United States. Most recently, the federal labs have played an important role in combating the COVID-19 pandemic by providing data, publications, medical expertise, research, technologies, and supercomputing capabilities to accelerate understanding, diagnosis, and treatment of the disease, as well as the development of a vaccine.[2]

---

[1] In addition to providing extramural funding, the U.S. government contributed to the HGP by providing curation and storage of genomic data within GenBank, operated by the National Center for Biotechnology Information (NCBI), part of the National Library of Medicine at NIH. GenBank originated in Los Alamos National Laboratory in the 1970s (Contreras, 2017).
[2] DOE laboratories are part of the COVID-19 High Performance Computing Consortium, which is providing supercomputing systems to researchers for use in addressing the epidemiological, bioinformatics, and molecular modeling needs of the COVID-19 response (OSTP, 2020).

THE FEDERAL LABORATORY INFRASTRUCTURE

The current U.S. federal laboratory infrastructure consists of more than 300 labs that range from small, off-site facilities with staff of 10 or fewer scientists to sprawling complexes with thousands of scientists, engineers, and support personnel (Hughes et al., 2011). In fiscal year 2016, the federal labs accounted for 38 percent ($43.4 billion) of federal obligations for research and development (R&D) (more than $115 billion) (NIST, 2019a). Four agencies (DOD, DOE, the Department of Health and Human Services [HHS], and NASA) accounted for nearly 90 percent of the total federal lab expenditures (NIST, 2019a).

Eleven federal agencies have significant lab operations: the Department of Agriculture (USDA), the Department of Commerce (DOC), DOD, DOE, HHS, the Department of Homeland Security (DHS), the Department of the Interior (DOI), the Department of Transportation (DOT), the Department of Veterans Affairs (VA), the Environmental Protection Agency (EPA), and NASA. There is substantial variation across the laboratories—even within agencies and individual laboratories—with respect to their mission, culture, size, management, types of research, and types of output.[3]

GOVERNMENT-OWNED, GOVERNMENT-OPERATED (GOGO) AND GOVERNMENT-OWNED, CONTRACTOR-OPERATED (GOCO) LABORATORIES

Federal laboratories are a mix of GOGOs and GOCOs, which are governed by different legislative and regulatory schemes. These legislative and regulatory differences have resulted in a number of institutional differences with respect to the nature of operations, personnel obligations, and approaches to private-sector engagement related to technology transfer and commercialization, differences that reflect the priorities and constraints of the respective legislative and regulatory authorities (Snyder and Thomas, 2014; Hughes et al., 2011; Link et al., 2019).

GOGO laboratories are owned or leased by the federal government, and their personnel are considered federal employees. GOCO laboratories, on the other hand, are owned and equipped by the federal government but operated under contract by for-profit companies, nonprofit companies, and universities, either on their own or in consortia, and their personnel are not considered federal employees. Some GOCO laboratories are designated as FFRDCs, public–private partnerships that conduct research for the U.S. government. As of this writing, 12 federal agencies sponsor a total of 42 FFRDCs.

The different policy frameworks for GOGOs and GOCOs define the suite of legal tools available to secure, manage, share, and transfer digital

---

[3] A detailed discussion of the history and implications of these structural differences among federal labs is beyond the scope of this report.

innovations created by the federal labs where relevant. For example, both GOGOs and GOCOs are eligible to patent and license inventions, but only GOCOs that have secured the permission of their respective responsible agency are eligible to claim copyright protection.[4]

OVERVIEW OF THE RESEARCH ACTIVITIES OF THE FEDERAL LABORATORIES

The activities of federal laboratories vary widely, driven in part by agency missions and priorities and the types of research (basic or applied) and development they conduct. The labs' mission activities also are driven by congressional appropriations, and their disparate missions may affect the propensity or ability of the private sector to use their research outputs in commercial products. Additionally, the nature of research conducted at the federal labs can range from open/unclassified, to restricted, to classified. Restricted and classified research, which have national security implications, generally are not transferred to the private sector.

The HHS labs vary greatly in mission and focus. Some NIH labs are engaged in fundamental research, while the NIH Clinical Center conducts more than 1,000 clinical studies each year to help transfer laboratory discoveries into routine use as patient treatments. The Food and Drug Administration's intramural research program spans a range of sectors and functional utilities—from the development of animal models and tools to assessments of emergency medical equipment. Similarly, NASA operates labs with diverse missions that include supporting human spaceflight, developing space operations and related systems, testing the safety and efficiency of hardware, providing preflight training facilities, and conducting ground-based analog studies and furthering understanding of human responses to space travel.

Often, moreover, a single agency may have multiple missions. For example, the DOD labs conduct R&D in support of the national defense, with each service branch (Air Force, Army, Navy) operating several labs to meet its mission needs. Even a single lab can have multiple missions and multiple areas of focus for its research program. An example is the Idaho National Laboratory (INL), which conducts basic and applied nuclear and radiological science research, pursues developments in nuclear power, and evaluates new battery technologies for electric-drive vehicles, among other areas of focus.[5]

---

[4] Intellectual property issues pertaining to federal labs are discussed in greater detail in Chapters 4 and 5.
[5] See INL Overview at https://factsheets.inl.gov/Shared%20Documents/overview.pdf#search=bas ic%20research.

TECHNOLOGY TRANSFER LEGISLATION AND POLICY RELEVANT TO FEDERAL LABORATORIES

Throughout the 1980s, Congress and the executive branch expanded cooperation among federal laboratories, academia, and industry in an effort to derive more value from federally funded R&D. The federal policy framework for the labs consists of several key pieces of legislation aimed at enhancing technology transfer of their innovations, including digital products.

The first key legislation is the Stevenson-Wydler Technology Innovation Act of 1980 (Pub. L. No. 96-480), which recognizes that "many new discoveries and advances in science occur in universities and federal laboratories" and encourages "cooperation among academia, federal laboratories, labor, and industry" through such mechanisms as "technology transfer, personnel exchange, joint research projects, and others" (Pub. L. No. 96-480).[6] The act also mandates the creation of an Office of Research and Technology Applications (ORTA) at each lab with 200 or more technical staff to facilitate technology transfers,[7] which the respective responsible agencies are required to fund.[8] In addition, the act sets a cap on annual royalty awards (currently $150,000) for researchers at the federal labs.[9]

Second is the Bayh-Dole Act of 1980 (Pub. L. No. 96-517), which governs intellectual property for inventions developed with federal government funds. That act fundamentally changed the nation's system of technology transfer by allowing contractors supported by the federal agencies to own such inventions and to issue exclusive licenses on those patents under certain conditions (see Chapter 4).[10]

Third is the Federal Technology Transfer Act of 1986 (FTTA) (Pub. L. No. 99-502), which amended the Stevenson-Wydler Act to strengthen technology transfer from the federal labs by providing that "technology transfer, consistent with mission responsibilities, is a responsibility of each laboratory science and engineering professional" (15 U.S.C. § 3701[a][2]), requiring technology transfer to be considered in employee evaluations (15 U.S.C. § 3701[a][3]), and establishing a principle of royalty sharing for federal inventors (15 U.S.C. § 3710c[a][1][a][i]). Passage of this legislation fortified the government's focus on maximizing the value of federally funded technology through its utilization in real-world applications. The act's royalty payment requirements were extended to nongovernmental employees at federal labs in the Omnibus Trade and Competitiveness Act of 1988 (Pub. L. No. 100-418; 15 U.S.C. § 3710[b]). In addition, the FTTA created a new technology transfer mechanism, the cooperative

---

[6] 15 U.S.C. § 3701 et seq.
[7] 15 U.S.C. § 3701.
[8] 15 U.S.C. § 3710(b).
[9] The National Technology Transfer and Advancement Act of 1995, Pub. L. No. 104-113, raised the cap from $100,000 to $150,000.
[10] 35 U.S.C. 209(e).

research and development agreement (CRADA), for GOGO labs. CRADAs enable the labs to engage in cooperative research with federal agencies, state or local governments, industry, and nonprofits—including universities—and to enter into advance agreements with businesses for patent acquisition or licensing rights to inventions resulting from the CRADA.[11] The FTTA also allows current and former federal employees to participate in commercial development as long as there are no conflicts of interest (15 U.S.C. § 3710[a][b][3][c]).

In 1987, President Ronald Reagan issued Executive Order 12591—"Facilitating Access to Science and Technology"—which encouraged GOGO labs "to enter into [CRADAs] with other federal laboratories, state and local governments, universities, and the private sector" (52 Fed. Reg. 13414, 3 C.F.R., 1987 Comp., p. 220). It also established the Technology Exchange of Scientists and Engineers program, which allows government scientists to accept temporary assignments in the private sector and private-sector researchers to do the same at federal labs.

The National Competitiveness Technology Transfer Act of 1989 (Pub. L. No. 101-189) gave GOCO labs the authority to enter into CRADAs under terms similar to those that applied to GOGO labs. Subsequently, the National Technology Transfer and Advancement Act of 1995 (Pub. L. No. 104-113) provided that a CRADA partner collaborating with either a GOCO or a GOGO lab would, at a minimum, receive a nonexclusive license to any inventions arising from the collaboration.

There are other laws and policies that have an indirect impact on technology transfer from the federal labs. For example, export control laws restrict the dissemination of certain research developments and technical data generated by the labs. The Export Controls Reform Act of 2018 (Title XVII, Subtitle B of Pub. L. No. 115-232) directs DOC to establish export controls on "emerging and foundational technologies" essential to U.S. national security. DOC issued its first such regulation in January 2020, imposing controls on a specific application of artificial intelligence that would train neural networks to analyze geospatial imagery.[12]

Finally, with regard to tracking outcomes, the Technology Transfer Commercialization Act of 2000 (Pub. L. No. 106-404) revised the technology transfer reporting requirements for federal agencies, requiring that they submit an annual report to the Office of Management and Budget summarizing their

---

[11] CRADAs are codified in 15 U.S.C. § 3710(a), in which they are defined as "...any agreement between one or more Federal laboratories and one or more non-Federal parties under which the Government, through its laboratories, provides personnel, services, facilities, equipment, intellectual property or other resources with or without reimbursement (but not funds to non-Federal parties) and the non-Federal parties provide funds, personnel, services, facilities, equipment, intellectual property, or other resources toward the conduct of specified research or development efforts which are consistent with the missions of the laboratory...."

[12] 15 C.F.R. Part 774 (Docket No. 191217–0116) R.I.N. 0694–AH89 Addition of Software Specially Designed to Automate the Analysis of Geospatial Imagery to the Export Control Classification Number 0Y521 Series, *Federal Register* Vol. 85, No. 3, pp. 459–462 (January 2020).

technology transfer activities. These reporting requirements are discussed in greater detail in Chapter 7.

CONCLUSION

Over the years, Congress and the executive branch have sought to reduce barriers to and promote partnerships between and among federal laboratories, academia, and industry. Positioned between industry and academia, federal labs play a unique role in these partnerships with respect to time scale, risk tolerance, facilities, and the size of the research teams. Today, a growing network of institutional arrangements is focused on enabling the transfer of federally funded research and innovation to benefit society. Federal labs—both GOGO and GOCO—possess scientific expertise that, together with their sophisticated, world-class scientific facilities, makes them crucial national resources for scientific discoveries, technological innovation, and education.

3

Digital Products and Federal Policy for the Innovation Economy

Digital output from federal laboratories includes data, metadata, images, software, code, tools, databases, algorithms, and statistical models. These digital products can be copied at little or no cost and used by many without limit or additional cost. Given that digital products are produced by federal labs, are paid for with taxpayer dollars, and can generate large positive externalities, policies that foster their widespread use and rapid dissemination yield a large societal benefit. Society can often benefit most when technology is in the public domain freely, which in theory makes the assets freely available to all firms. However, small and minority-owned firms can be systemically excluded from accessing or exploiting what is in the public domain because of a lack of resources or the structure of the specific markets in which they operate. Moreover, when substantial investment capital and expenditures are necessary to bring a digital invention to market and otherwise promote its use by the public, and that investment would not be recoverable in a competitive market, some form of exclusivity may be required to create incentives for the investment.

DIGITAL PRODUCTS AND INNOVATION

Innovation has enabled capabilities in data collection, computation, simulation, and analysis unheard of even a decade ago. Numerous fields, from science to cybersecurity and city management to transportation, benefit from and are continuously challenged by rapidly evolving digital innovation.

Digital products power nearly every facet of modern life. Increased computational power, artificial intelligence (AI), and machine learning (ML) are driving pathbreaking progress in science and medicine. AI and ML, for example, are helping to make society "smarter," whether by incorporating crash avoidance technology into automobiles, building more efficient energy management systems for homes and utilities, or using facial recognition technologies to combat terrorism. Further, open-source software (OSS) and open data have become integral components of the modern technological infrastructure. Use of OSS is widespread among industry, academia, and the federal government, enabling a broad community of developers to collaborate on new, innovative technologies.

Looking beyond the information and communications technology (ICT) sector, digital technology also features prominently in the immense health care and biomedical research enterprise. Today, digital products anchor efforts to deploy health care, maintain medical records, conduct biomedical research, and discover new drugs and therapies. The Human Genome Project (HGP), for example, a massive international undertaking to sequence the entire genome of the human species, released all of the data it generated into the public domain, creating new industries virtually overnight. Bioinformatics, genetic diagnostics, pharmacogenomics, and precision medicine all have their roots in data produced and released by this and subsequent genomic data projects. As noted by the National Science Foundation (NSF), industries that produce products and services for the digital economy have some of the highest innovation rates in the country, ranging from software publishing (61 percent), to computer and electronic products manufacturing (53 percent), to medical equipment and supplies (44 percent), to scientific research and development (R&D) services (43 percent).[1]

INTELLECTUAL PROPERTY POLICY AND INNOVATION IN THE FEDERAL LABORATORIES

When examining the laws and policies that specifically govern the development of digital products from the federal laboratories, it is useful first to take a step back and consider the overall framework of innovations arising from the federal lab system. The interaction of two foundational premises—the role of government in creating public resources and the role of intellectual property (IP) law in incentivizing innovation—anchors the function of the labs in the national economy and is essential to understanding the basis for IP regulation within the labs.

As discussed in Chapter 2, federal labs were established to conduct research in key sectors (for example, the agricultural experiment stations for agriculture), to assist in developing industry-wide standards, or to develop defense-related technologies (such as radar and the atomic bomb). These are classic public resources, designed to benefit the nation as a whole and funded by taxpayers. After World War II, the federal lab system expanded to encompass further civilian applications, such as nuclear power, space exploration, and medical research. In each of these cases, the role of the labs was to create some welfare-enhancing technology or to generate new knowledge, which would be deployed for the public benefit. As with other types of infrastructural assets, these public resources generated significant spillover effects in terms of commercial applications not pursued directly by government agencies.

---

[1] Percentages of U.S. companies in a particular industry reporting "product or process innovation" in the period 2014–2016 (NSB and NSF, 2020).

Yet by the 1970s, U.S. policy makers recognized that potentially useful technologies developed within government labs were not finding their way into commercial products and that the United States lagged behind its allies in transferring federally created technology to the private sector. For example, Japan's Ministry of International Trade and Industry, which formulates Japanese industrial policy, directed significant resources to the successful development of such market sectors as consumer electronics and automobiles using technology initially developed in national labs. Thus the U.S. Congress recognized the need for a way to increase the commercialization of technologies developed by the federal government and began developing a series of policies for this purpose, including policies relating to IP for products developed with federal funds. Studies of the impact of the Bayh-Dole Act, which transferred ownership of inventions and IP arising from publicly funded research from federal agencies to universities showed that university ownership of IP rights did not have a detrimental impact on commercialization (NRC, 2011). See Box 3-1 for more information on the Bayh-Dole Act.

Federal IP policy also plays a role in incentivizing innovation in the private sector. Article I, Section 8, Clause 8 of the U.S. Constitution states that Congress is authorized to enact patent and copyright laws "to promote the progress of science and useful arts"—an unbridled instrumentalist justification for IP. It authorizes Congress to grant limited periods of exclusivity to "authors and inventors" to incentivize "progress"—the creation of new works. In other words,

---

BOX 3-1
The Bayh-Dole Act

Prior to the passage of the Patent and Trademark Law Amendments Act of 1980 (also known as the Bayh-Dole Act), there was a lack of consistency and clarity about intellectual property rights for inventions funded by federal agencies, with some agencies claiming the intellectual property they had funded and others giving the rights to their extramural grantees (Contreras, 2021). The Bayh-Dole Act allowed nonprofit research organizations and small businesses to claim ownership of, and the right to patent, their federally funded discoveries. In 2011, a National Academies study found that the system put in place by the Bayh-Dole Act "is unquestionably more effective than its predecessor system" (NRC, 2011, p. 3). That study also found that there was little evidence that "IP considerations interfere with other important avenues of transferring research results to development and commercial use" (NRC, 2011, p. 3). The act imposed conditions on disclosure and some controls on these extramural awardees, such as giving the federal funding agency the right to use the invention and allowing the federal government to grant licenses to third parties if the grantee has not sufficiently exploited the invention ("march-in rights") (35 U.S.C. § 203). However, the controls placed on extramural awardees do not include ensuring that licenses are in the public interest, although the act does impose domestic manufacturing requirements on potential licensees (35 U.S.C. § 204).

exclusivity may be granted to the extent that it promotes innovation. Without exclusive rights, incentives for firms to invest in innovation tend to be considerably reduced because of the possibility of free rider effects (Heller and Eisenberg, 1998; Buchanan and Yoon, 2000). Conversely, if granting exclusivity would not promote innovation, it should not be granted. This is the case because works the public can freely utilize and adapt also lead to innovation, as demonstrated by the significant advances achieved through OSS and works dedicated largely to the public domain, such as the Internet and the Global Positioning System (GPS) signal.

At the same time, the government may need to assert some control over the use of digital products generated by federal labs. For example, free distribution of digital technologies might encourage and enhance the ability of non-U.S. entities to invest in and develop those same technologies, in competition with U.S. firms. Free distribution might also hinder the government from exerting downstream controls over innovations produced from the digital technologies, including providing transparency of product or pricing information to the public or restricting anticompetitive behaviors (Okediji, 2016). Finally, there is evidence that such factors as gender, race, and appearance affect the ability of a scientist to commercialize new inventions (Dolmans et al., 2016; Shane et al., 2015). And there is evidence that social dimensions, including differences in resources, economic disparities, and gender or racial discrimination, affect an individual's ability to take advantage of resources, such as digital technologies, that are placed in the public domain (Chander and Sunder, 2004; Veletsianos and Kimmons, 2012; Willinsky, 2006).

In short, acting in the public interest will require balancing a variety of factors to determine when government stewardship is best accomplished by allowing exclusive use by a firm, by the adoption of open-access licensing, or by dedication to the public domain (with or without a license) to advance scientific progress and innovation.

Bringing Federal Technologies into the Marketplace

The private sector plays an essential role in bringing federal technologies into the marketplace. Federal laboratories are neither well suited nor chartered to commercialize their work products directly, being driven by the missions of the agencies with which they are associated rather than market forces. Therefore, technology transfer from federal labs to the commercial marketplace is possible only through partnerships with private actors and measures to meet the need for economic incentives that make such partnerships feasible.

Clearly, some products of federal labs, such as U.S. Geological Survey (USGS) data, the GPS signal, and the human genome sequence, can be used by the private sector with minimal adaptation. Commercial firms, each of which has access to the same federally provisioned no-cost inputs, can then compete on the basis of their proprietary improvements on and applications using those inputs (e.g., navigation software, weather prediction systems, diagnostic kits, and genetically tailored drugs). However, not all products of federal labs can be translated directly, and without significant additional investment, into commercial products; some may require augmentation, adaptation, or modification to become commercially viable. Successfully commercialized software also can require significant investment in user support, upgrades, and maintenance.

Intellectual Property Rights Considerations

Government decisions related to IP rights (IPRs) in federal technology need to take into account the likelihood that the technology can be commercialized absent exclusivity, or costly adaptations may be required that would justify granting an IPR. For example, if the total expected market for the adapted product (i.e., when offered by a single source without competition) would yield net profit in excess of the cost of making the necessary adaptations, the grant of exclusivity may be justified for that product. This is the case, however, only if commercialization of the federal product would not otherwise occur in a market under normal competitive conditions.[2] Otherwise, granting that private actor the exclusive right to exploit the federal product would operate simply as a wealth transfer to the private actor facilitated by the federal government, with no offsetting welfare benefit. Such wealth transfers, absent other welfare gains, are to be avoided by government agencies. Admittedly, moreover, it is difficult to predict in any given instance how much it will cost to adapt a particular federal technology for commercial use, whether that product would be commercialized without exclusivity, whether it will be successful in the marketplace, what costs will be involved in maintaining and supporting it, and whether patent or copyright rights for that product would eventually be recognized by a court.

The National Institutes of Health (NIH) has developed best practices for its laboratories with regard to the patenting and licensing of genomic inventions. These practices include avoiding exclusivity for "broad enabling technologies" that would be most beneficial if "widely available and accessible to the scientific community" (NIH, 2005). By the same token, if a federal technology would be broadly beneficial to society, granting exclusive rights to a single firm should be avoided unless it is necessary to ensure that the technology is commercialized.

Another relevant factor to consider is the ultimate cost that will be borne by members of the public to access and use the federal product. According to the so-called "double subsidy" argument, U.S. taxpayers should have free access to work funded by tax dollars; allowing a private actor to privatize a public good results in a double charge to the taxpayers. But in contrast, some critics have observed that releasing federal products to the public gives access not only to the U.S. taxpayers who funded that work but also to foreign users, which raises two separate issues. First, these foreign users did not contribute to the creation of U.S.

---

[2] As discussed in Chapter 6, the Department of Energy, the National Institutes of Health, and the National Aeronautics and Space Administration have introduced programs to improve technology transfer of inventions created at the federal labs.

taxpayer investments. Second, giving foreign firms access to U.S.-created digital products enables them to compete with American businesses, an outcome that appears to be at odds with the goals of the Stevenson-Wydler Act.

Even so, as discussed further below, federal policy favors disseminating the results of scientific endeavors as widely as possible. Accordingly, scientists in most federal labs are encouraged to publish their research in scientific journals and other publications, which many do. The publications of scientists employed by government-owned, government-operated (GOGO) federal labs are a significant form of knowledge transfer and are generally not subject to copyright restrictions. However, the underlying invention, if any, described in the published article may be the subject of a patent or copyright. Chapters 4 and 5 describe the IP issues related to federal labs in more detail.

Table 3-1 summarizes the analysis outlined in this section at a high level using paradigmatic examples of each technology type.[3] When an unclassified federal technology is readily adaptable to commercial use without significant expenditure, as in the case of genomic data, that federal technology should achieve the broadest dissemination and yield the greatest welfare gains when it is treated as a public resource accessible to and usable by all. Likewise, when a federal technology is adaptable to commercial use with only modest expenditures, as in the case of a software program that was designed for use in a government setting but can be adapted to a commercial setting with modest programming modifications, treating the technology as a public resource (e.g., through OSS release or dedication to the public domain) is likely to lead to its broadest dissemination and use. In contrast, a federal technology, such as certain types of health care software that require approval from the Food and Drug Administration

TABLE 3-1 Nature, Recommended Treatment, and Examples of Federal Laboratory Technologies

Nature of Federal Technology	Recommended Treatment	Paradigmatic Examples
Commercially usable without adaptation	Publicly available	Scientific data
Commercially usable with modest adaptation	Publicly available	Research tools
Commercially usable with significant/costly adaptation, and commercialization will not occur under market competition	Limited exclusivity	Certain types of health software

---

[3] A more detailed set of considerations used by federal labs in deciding whether to release a particular software product on an OSS basis is described in Chapter 6.

that would require substantial expenditure before commercialization may require some degree of exclusivity if it is to be commercialized successfully.

In general, the application of IP law to the federal labs has, over the years, been inconsistent and lacking in a single set of guiding principles. This situation likely reflects a combination of historical accident, uncoordinated decision making across a range of agencies and legal domains, and the accumulation of special-purpose exceptions (some directed by Congress) that have persisted over the years. As described in Chapters 4 and 5, the result is that the landscape of IP for federal labs today is difficult to catalog and address through any single set of policy prescriptions.

THE ECONOMICS OF DIGITAL PRODUCTS

The framework described above is generally agnostic to the underlying technology in question and relies instead on the technology's "usability" factor. It is important to note, however, that digital products differ in important ways from their tangible counterparts, and it is worth examining the economic theory behind them to see whether the above framework still applies. Digital products, unlike physical products, are distinguished by their "nonrival" nature, which means they have nearly zero costs of reproduction, and multiple users can share them at no additional cost. As with all products that fall within the IP domain, digital products typically have substantial fixed or "first-copy" costs. Once they have been created, however, the cost of making them available to another user (the "marginal cost") is often negligible.

The near-zero reproduction cost or nonrival nature of digital products means that maximizing their availability can yield large economic and societal benefits. When it costs virtually nothing to serve another consumer, charging for a product can result in inefficiency. Of course, it is possible to generate revenue by selling (or otherwise monetizing, such as via advertising) digital products, as commercial firms do.

Unlike firms, which generate revenue from digital products in order to survive, federal laboratories do not need to generate royalties and licensing revenue to fund their operations.[4] As discussed above, most commercially relevant digital products generated by federal labs are by-products of the labs' mission-driven research activity. Moreover, these digital products are financed by taxpayers, which constitutes an additional rationale for making them openly and freely available. Indeed, many digital products developed by the federal labs are freely distributed via repositories of open data, open code, and open publications (see Chapter 7 for more information). At the same time, as observed earlier, evidence suggests that some users are not in a position (because of their limited capabilities or the competitive structure of the specific industry) to easily

---

[4] As discussed Chapter 6, a small share of federal labs fund their technology transfer offices out of licensing and royalty revenue.

determine how to access and use what is in the public domain (Chander and Sunder, 2004; Veletsianos and Kimmons, 2012; Willinsky, 2006).

Although the nonrivalrous nature of government digital products suggests that charging for them can create inefficiency, there can be situations in which alternatives to open availability can better advance development. For example, it is possible that some digital products created in federal labs are not directly usable off the shelf and require such substantial additional commercial investment that only a sole licensee would garner commercial returns adequate to cover the cost of that investment.

It also is possible that market actors will not partner with the federal labs without securing exclusive rights to the products created through the partnership. If multiple competitors have access to the same underlying federal technology and the ultimate product is readily imitable, none of them may be able to capture sufficient revenue when the product is sold to justify the initial expenditure required to develop and commercialize the technology. As a result, *no* private actor may have a sufficient economic incentive to commercialize the federal product, and it will remain uncommercialized, yielding no social benefits whatsoever. Researchers have shown, at least in the case of university technology transfer, that exclusive licenses may be required to induce firms to invest in the development of embryonic inventions (Buchanan and Yoon, 2000; Colyvas et al., 2002; Heller and Eisenberg, 1998; Mowery et al., 2001; Thursby and Thursby, 2007). A variety of examples illustrating this effect have been reported to the Government Accountability Office and repeated at various Congressional hearings, although the extent of these circumstances is unknown. These examples included "a computer program that would assist dermatologists in prescribing medications and other treatments for medical problems, such as acne" (GAO, 1991, p. 4); software that allows researchers to capture vehicle performance data during an emissions and fuel economy test (U.S. House, 1992, p. 33); and software "to maximize cotton yields in the southern United States by assisting farmers in deciding, for example, when to irrigate, fertilize, and defoliate their cotton crops" (GAO, 1990, p. 32). The committee received evidence of the need for IP protection for certain products, such as software for instrumentation, to aid in commercialization.[5]

Finally, while federal labs may develop software that offers the *potential* for commercial application, that potential may not be realized without significant codevelopment effort on the part of both lab and industry personnel, necessitating investment on the part of industry partners. In such a circumstance, it is no longer the government that bears the full cost of technology development. One example of this situation presented to the committee was a cooperative research agreement between Los Alamos National Laboratory (LANL) and the consumer goods company Procter & Gamble (P&G).[6] In that case, P&G asked for help to improve product reliability, and LANL responded by developing a new (and unproven)

---

[5] Presentation to the committee by Mark Rohrbaugh, National Institutes of Health, December 5, 2019.
[6] Presentation to committee by Art Koehler, Procter & Gamble, December 6, 2019.

statistical model that could be used to simulate changes to production lines. To test this model, P&G had to collect and feed to the model real-world data, and once proven, the model had to be translated into a user-friendly "toolbox" that could be used across the company. The use of collaborative efforts with industry, discussed in Chapter 6, suggests that the need for such codevelopment is common. The general principle guiding the conferring of control rights from the government initially is whether, absent such control rights, a private actor would have sufficient incentive to build upon and develop the data or software in question for societal benefit.

CONCLUSION

In conclusion, there can be important exceptions to the argument that digital products produced in federal laboratories should be made available to private firms with no exclusivity restrictions and no charge. The criteria for making those exceptions are discussed further in Chapters 4 and 5.

FINDINGS AND RECOMMENDATIONS

Finding 3-1: Making government data freely and openly available maximizes the use, reuse, and therefore the value of these data for commercial and noncommercial entities.

Finding 3-2: Federally produced digital products often yield large societal benefits when widely distributed, although federal laboratories may need to restrict access to those products when significant and costly follow-on development by firms is needed to commercialize them.

Finding 3-3: While placing digital products in the public domain may reduce obstacles to their use, reliance on the public domain alone will not enable the participation of small firms, minority-owned firms, woman-owned firms, and members of society that lack the market networks, resources, and tools to discover and exploit what is available in the public domain.

Recommendation 3-1: Federal laboratory directors should ensure that data and associated metadata produced by their labs are freely and openly available for use by individuals, researchers, and firms to the fullest extent possible under existing statutes and policies.

Recommendation 3-2: When additional substantial investment by the private sector is necessary to commercialize a digital innovation and the ultimate product is readily imitable, a federal laboratory director should allow exclusive access to that innovation to incentivize such investment.

Recommendation 3-3: Federal laboratory directors should consider ways to identify and support small, minority-owned, and woman-owned firms and members of society that may not be in a position to identify freely available digital goods, may not know how to interface with the federal labs on such matters, and/or may not understand how the use of these digital products may be relevant to their interests. Federal lab directors should proactively address such disparities in access.

4

Patents, Trade Secrets, Digital Products, and Federal Laboratories

As discussed in Chapter 3, digital products created by federal laboratories may be eligible for different forms of intellectual property rights (IPRs). Article I, Section 8, Clause 8 of the U.S. Constitution authorizes Congress to enact patent and copyright laws "To promote the progress of science and useful arts"—a clear instrumentalist justification. It empowers Congress to grant limited periods of exclusivity to "authors and inventors" to promote "progress," understood to include the creation of new works. This chapter examines federal labs' use of patents and trade secrets for digital products and the impact on the dissemination and commercialization of those products. Noted in the discussion is that many valuable digital products created by federal labs lack formal IP protection and that labs may compensate for this lack of legal protection by imposing restrictive contractual terms and technological control mechanisms on those products.

PATENTS

Historically, patents have been a primary tool utilized by federal laboratories to protect inventions and license rights to those inventions to the private sector. Beginning with a historical overview of the use of patents for digital products, this section describes federal practices and policies with respect to such products developed with the involvement of federal labs and offers a brief discussion of federal labs' reporting on patents.

History of Patents on Digital Products

A primary goal of patent law is to encourage and enhance innovation and the commercialization of new technologies. Patent protection is possible only when an inventor applies for and is granted a patent by the U.S. Patent and Trademark Office (USPTO), a process that tends to be expensive, complex, difficult, and time-consuming. In most cases, digital content, audiovisual works, data, and the like do not qualify as patentable subject matter, but there are exceptions. This section looks at two types of digital products that have generated significant controversy with respect to patenting: software and algorithms, and scientific and technical data.

Software and Algorithms

The patent eligibility of computer software and algorithms has fluctuated over time. It has long been the case that abstract ideas, such as mathematical formulae, are not eligible as patent subject matter. In Gottschalk v. Benson, 403 U.S. 63 (1972), the Supreme Court rejected a patent claiming "a method for converting binary-coded-decimal...numerals into pure binary numerals" using a general-purpose digital computer. The Court reasoned that the "claim is so abstract and sweeping as to cover both known and unknown uses of the...conversion [method]." As a result, the claim was considered to consist of abstract ideas that were ineligible for patent protection. Six years later, in Parker v. Flook, 437 U.S. 584 (1978), the Court held that a patent claiming several conventional applications of a novel mathematical formula was similarly drawn to ineligible subject matter.

It was not until 1981, in Diamond v. Diehr, 450 U.S. 175 (1981), that the Supreme Court upheld a patent claiming computer software. The claimed method employed the well-known Arrhenius equation to calculate and control the temperature in a process for curing rubber. The Court held that while the Arrhenius equation itself was not patentable, the claimed method for curing rubber was an industrial process of a type that has historically enjoyed patent protection. The use of the equation and a computer were incidental to the patentable inventive process.

Although the requirements for patenting software fluctuated over the next three decades, large numbers of such patents were issued. Software patents differ substantially from copyrights covering computer software. Copyright protects the expression of a work—the lines of code written by a programmer, the executable version of that code, and the screen displays and images generated by the code. Patents, on the other hand, protect software functionality at a higher level. Actual source code is seldom included in a patent application. In principle, the disclosure requirements of patent law counsel that flowcharts showing the logical structure of a program should be included (Rai, 2012). Given the severe time limitations faced by patent examiners, however, their enforcement of patentability requirements is often subpar (Frakes and Wasserman, 2017), and courts have not enforced the principle that software disclosure requires something more than high-level, generalized information about the functions accomplished (but see Allison and Ouellette, 2016). As a consequence, software patents in many cases simply describe and claim the functions accomplished by particular programs (Lemley, 2013).

The vagueness, potential overbreadth, and overall poor quality of many software patents led to significant criticism of software patenting in the 2000s. Notorious examples of questionable software patents emerged, including Amazon's "one-click shopping" patent, British Telecom's patent that allegedly covered "the Internet," and Apple's patents covering such basic smartphone gestures as "tap to zoom." Compounding these issues, the 2000s also saw the rise of significant patent litigation initiated by so-called patent assertion (or nonpracticing) entities (known colloquially as "patent trolls") that took advantage of overly broad and vague patent claim language to seek monetary settlements from many firms in the electronics and computing industry. The patent system came under heavy fire from the popular media, scholars, and even the Obama Administration (Burk and Lemley, 2009; Bessen and Meurer, 2009; Rai, 2012, pp. 1274–1277; Executive Office of the President, 2013).

Perhaps in response to some of these issues, the Supreme Court again turned its attention to algorithmic patents in 2010. In Bilski v. Kappos, 561 U.S. 593 (2010), the Court invoked the requirement of patentable subject matter to hold that an algorithm for calculating a fixed price for monthly utility bills was an unpatentable abstract idea. Then, in Alice Corp. v. CLS Bank International, 573 U.S. 208 (2014), the Court rejected "patent claims drawn to a computer-implemented, electronic escrow service for facilitating financial transactions," holding that the invention was merely an abstract idea. The Court also observed that merely including a generic computer implementation of such an abstract idea fails to transform it into a patent-eligible invention.

The holding in *Alice* overturned much existing wisdom and practice regarding software patenting. The holding appears to have led, at least initially, to a steep increase in the number of cases in which patent or patent application claims for software and related digital products, particularly in the area of software covering business methods, were found to be invalid (Tran, 2016; Chien and Wu, 2018).[1] Many in the patent bar and judiciary have argued that the standard that was set in *Alice* is overly ambiguous and indeterminate (Reinecke, 2019).

Because of definitional challenges, rigorous empirical assessment of the longer-term impact of *Alice* on software patenting is difficult. Over the course of the decades-long controversy surrounding software patents detailed above, researchers attempting to examine this question have used differing definitions for software, and their results have differed substantially based on the definition used (Rai et al., 2009). In 2013, the Office of the Chief Economist at the USPTO, working with patent examiners, developed a definition of software based on USPTO classifications, which is used in this report (Graham and Vishnubhakat, 2013). But this definition is far from definitive. Because software is a "general-purpose" technology, now utilized in many if not most areas of invention, distinguishing "pure" software capable of performing on many platforms from

---

[1] Also contributing to this increase was the introduction in 2012 of a new procedure for challenging patents at the Patent Trial and Appeals Board (PTAB), known as *inter partes* review.

software inextricably linked to a hardware product can be difficult (Rai et al., 2009).

Categorization issues aside, one industry source that purports to utilize the 2013 Graham/Vishnubhakat definition reports that by 2019, more than 60 percent of all newly issued U.S. patents covered software-related inventions (Millien, 2020). In addition, perhaps because of USPTO guidance and Federal Circuit decisions that interpret *Alice* narrowly, the number of successful challenges to software claims appears to have declined in the years immediately after the *Alice* decision was rendered (Saltiel, 2019; Tran and Benevento, 2019). Thus, patenting activity in the sector continues.

Scientific and Technical Data

The federal government has made, and continues to make, large quantities of scientific data available to the public. Typical government-generated data, such as those describing astronomical, geological, and meteorological observations, are not considered to be useful inventions or discoveries that are eligible for patent protection.[2] In some cases, however, scientific and technical data can be closely linked to physical materials or processes and may thus be claimed as part of a patented invention.[3]

Attempts to include scientific data in patent claims have probably attracted the greatest attention in the area of human genomics. DNA is an organic molecule comprising two intertwined chains of four nucleotide bases (cytosine [C], guanine [G], adenine [A], and thymine [T]), a sugar called deoxyribose, and a phosphate group. One of DNA's principal functions within cells is to code for proteins, a function that is dictated by the precise order in which the nucleotide bases occur within segments of the DNA molecule known as genes. Thus, while genes and other DNA segments are organic molecules, the information conveyed by their nucleotide sequences has significant importance and commercial value.

Accordingly, by the late 1980s, researchers began to seek patents claiming DNA sequence information (Eisenberg, 1990; NRC, 2006). As technological capacity to sequence DNA increased, researchers appended voluminous sequence listings, often running more than 100 printed pages, to their patent applications. The growth of patents on human DNA sequences, often referred to as "gene patents," caused concern in some quarters, and by 2005, two Massachusetts Institute of Technology (MIT) researchers estimated that a full 20 percent of human genes were covered by patent claims to some degree (Jensen and Murray, 2005).

During this period, two significant legal developments limited the ability of researchers to patent DNA sequence information. The first arose under the

---

[2] In this sense, data should be distinguished from data structures, which have been recognized as eligible patent subject matter, at least prior to *Alice* (Hollander, 2003).
[3] The USPTO specifically provides instructions for including data tables, even those that may exceed 100 pages in length, in patent applications (MPEP § 608.05).

"utility" requirement of Section 101 of the Patent Act, which mandates that to be patentable, an invention must be "useful." As the rate of DNA sequences "discovered" in the laboratory increased, patent claims on such discoveries also increased. Yet in many cases, the precise biological function of these sequences was unknown, so it was not possible to describe their utility. Patent attorneys got around this obstacle by arguing that these sequences could be useful in further research as markers or locators for particular DNA segments. But by 1999, in response to significant criticism of such patents, the USPTO released draft Utility Guidelines that required inventions to have "specific, substantial, and credible" utility in order to be patented. This requirement became official USPTO policy in 2001, and was confirmed a few years later by the Federal Circuit in In re Fisher, 421 F.3d 1365 (2005).

The second major blow to DNA patenting was dealt by the Supreme Court in Association for Molecular Pathology v. Myriad Genetics, Inc., 569 U.S. 576 (2013). In that closely watched case, the Court held that the nucleotide sequences of the isolated and purified BRCA1/2 human genes were not patent-eligible subject matter, as they constituted naturally occurring substances found in every human cell. Thus, despite the patentee's insistence that its claims covered an organic molecule that in its isolated and purified form is found nowhere in nature, the Court reasoned that "the [patent] claims are not expressed in terms of chemical composition, nor do they rely on the chemical changes resulting from the isolation of a particular DNA section. Instead, they focus on the genetic *information* encoded in the BRCA1 and BRCA2 genes" (emphasis added). And in the Court's view, that information was not eligible for patent protection. Accordingly, DNA sequence data today are largely considered ineligible for patent protection.

Patents and Federal Digital Products

Federal laboratories have patented digital products for many years. This section reviews federal patenting practices and policies, first generally and then in connection with genomic data and software. It addresses both federally owned inventions and inventions owned by third parties but generated with contributions from federal researchers.

Patents Claiming Federal Inventions

In the United States, only an inventor(s) may apply for a patent on a particular invention. Typically, if an inventor is employed and the invention is within the scope of his or her employment, the inventor will assign ownership of the resulting patent to his or her employer. In contrast with the work-made-for-hire doctrine under copyright law, however, an employer does not automatically obtain ownership rights in inventions created by its employees.

Federal agencies may obtain ownership rights in inventions either through contractual assignments from their employees or contractors or by operation of law when a government-funded institution fails to make a disclosure or election to retain rights in an invention (35 U.S.C. § 202[c]).[4] Federal agencies are permitted to apply for, obtain, and maintain patents in the United States and foreign countries that claim inventions they own (35 U.S.C. § 207[a][1]). See Box 4-1 for more information on Section 209 of the Bayh-Dole Act.

Patents that arise from cooperative research and development agreements (CRADAs) (35 U.S.C. § 3710[a] et seq.) are another important category of patents closely tied to intramural research. Under the 1986 amendments to the Stevenson-Wydler Act, a federal laboratory that is a party to a CRADA may grant to its collaborating party an exclusive license or assignment for any inventions created by employees of the lab. However, these patents do not appear to be tracked under any existing reporting mechanism (see Chapter 7 for further discussion).

Genomic Data and Federal Patent Deterrence Strategies

Starting in 1991, researchers at the National Institutes of Health (NIH) began to file patent applications covering short DNA segments known as "expressed sequence tags" (ESTs), arguing that they could help locate much larger genes more quickly and efficiently than would sequencing the entire genome, making NIH one of the first agencies to seek patents on human DNA sequences. After some initial controversy, the agency abandoned its patenting efforts with respect to ESTs (IOM, 2003; Rai, 2012) and actively campaigned to have the USPTO amend its Utility Guidelines to disallow the patenting of DNA

BOX 4-1
Section 209 of the Bayh-Dole Act

Although the Bayh-Dole Act is usually discussed in the context of patenting by federally funded entities such as universities and small businesses, Sections 207–209 apply to patenting and licensing of inventions by the federal government. Specifically, Section 209 requires that federal agencies may grant an exclusive or partially exclusive license on a federally owned invention only if (1) granting the license is reasonable and necessary to bring the invention to practical application or promote its use by the public; (2) the public interest will be served; (3) the licensee makes a commitment to use the invention in a reasonable amount of time; (4) the granting of the license will not be anticompetitive; and (5) if the invention is covered by a foreign patent, the license will enhance U.S. industry in foreign commerce. Section 209 applies only to federally owned inventions and only to patented inventions, not copyrighted products.

---

[4] The provisions in question form part of the Bayh-Dole Act of 1980, Pub. L. No. 96-517, which is generally discussed in the context of patenting by federally funded universities and other institutions. However, §§ 207–209 of the act govern the patenting and licensing of inventions by federal agencies.

sequences of unknown function. This position eventually emerged in the USPTO's 1999 draft guidelines (NRC, 2006; Rai, 2012).

NIH opposition to DNA-based patents next manifested in the data release policies adopted during the Human Genome Project (HGP)—specifically, the adoption of the 1996 Bermuda Principles on data sharing as official agency policy. This policy required that genomic sequence data be released into NIH's GenBank or another public database within 24 hours of being generated, a significant commitment to public data sharing. This rapid, public release of HGP data not only represented the agency's disavowal of patenting but also was intended to deter third-party patenting by making the sequences prior art (Contreras, 2011).

In its 1996 policy adopting the Bermuda Principles, moreover, NIH warned that the agency "will monitor grantee activity…to learn whether or not attempts are being made to patent large blocks of primary human genomic DNA sequence" (NHGRI, 1996). And in its 2005 Best Practices for the Licensing of Genomic Inventions, the agency advised grantees to be cautious in seeking patents for DNA-based inventions (NIH, 2005). However, it is not clear that NIH has ever actively monitored or enforced compliance with these policies (Contreras, 2017; Rai and Eisenberg, 2003). The Bayh-Dole Act specifies a set of procedures for constraining patenting by grantees, and the NIH policies may accordingly have hortatory rather than legal significance.

Following the completion of the HGP in 2003, NIH continued to fund and curate ever-growing collections of genomic data (Contreras and Knoppers, 2018). As the types of data included in public databases grew more complex and began to encompass clinical, phenotypic, and demographic data, data access policies and procedures expanded to accommodate this new landscape. Through about 2008, NIH continued to insist upon rapid data release mechanisms that would limit the patentability of research data and discoveries. In more recent policies, however, the agency's advocacy for patent deterrence appears to have weakened, perhaps because since *Myriad*, patents no longer have posed a significant threat to the use of genomic data in research (Contreras and Knoppers, 2018). Further, despite NIH's overt opposition to patents covering raw DNA sequence data and its public release of large quantities of genomic data, the federal government remains a major holder of patents covering more specifically focused DNA-based inventions. According to one study, by 2005 the federal government held more DNA-based patents than any entity other than the University of California system (NRC, 2006), and as of 2009 it remained in fifth place (Cook-Deegan and Heaney, 2010).

Patenting of Software by Federal Laboratories

As discussed in Chapter 7, agency reporting of federal laboratory patents to the National Institute of Standards and Technology (NIST) does not identify the lab or whether the patent is for a digital product. Moreover, as noted above, defining what constitutes a software patent is difficult. Nonetheless, the committee attempted to gather as much data on this issue as possible.

Specifically, using the definition articulated by Graham and Vishnubhakat (2013), the committee examined software patenting between 1980 and 2014 by the Department of Energy (DOE), the Department of Defense (DOD), and the National Aeronautics and Space Administration (NASA). Starting in the 1990s, these three agencies began to secure a total of at least several hundred patents annually. Given that federal labs as a whole secure only a few thousand patents annually across all technologies, it appears that software patenting makes up a nontrivial percentage of the patent activity of federal labs.

That said, the committee's data encompass activity only through 2014, when the *Alice* case was decided by the Supreme Court. Accordingly, these data are consistent with the possibility, advanced by some federal lab representatives, that few labs currently seek software patents. Additionally, even the number of software patents sought and secured by federal labs pre-*Alice* may represent only a small percentage of the total software produced by the labs. As noted, the government releases a significant amount of software on an open-source basis.

Licensing of Inventions Generated with Federal Investment

Federal agencies are authorized to "grant nonexclusive, exclusive, or partially exclusive licenses under federally owned inventions, royalty-free or for royalties or other consideration, and on such terms and conditions...as determined appropriate in the public interest" (35 U.S.C. § 207[a][2]). Because the development of federal inventions was funded by U.S. taxpayers, such licenses are intended to benefit the U.S. economy.

Nonexclusive licenses, under which a patent holder grants the right to operate under a patent to multiple users, are generally viewed as favorable to broad dissemination of a given technology. NIH, for example, advises that "whenever possible, non-exclusive licensing should be pursued as a best practice" (NIH, 2005). An exclusive license, however, can provide the licensee with an incentive to make a significant financial investment in commercializing the licensed technology. As NIH notes, "in those cases where exclusive licensing is necessary to encourage research and development by private partners, best practices dictate that exclusive licenses should be appropriately tailored to ensure expeditious development of as many aspects of the technology as possible" (NIH, 2005). Contractual mechanisms for ensuring expeditious development include, among others, the imposition on the exclusive licensee of "diligence" milestones—commercial or technological goals that must be met within specified time periods, or the exclusivity or the license itself may be terminated. To this end, 35 U.S.C. § 209(b) establishes an expectation (though not a firm requirement) that exclusive licenses of federally developed technology shall "normally" be granted "only to a licensee who agrees that any products embodying the invention or produced through the use of the invention will be manufactured substantially in the United States."

If a federal agency wishes to grant a license that is exclusive or partially exclusive, 35 U.S.C. § 209(a) imposes a number of additional requirements on the agency; however, these requirements apply only to government-owned, government-operated (GOGO) labs. Specifically, (1) the exclusive license must be a "reasonable and necessary incentive to call forth the investment capital and expenditures needed to bring the invention to practical application or otherwise promote the invention's utilization by the public"; (2) the public must be served by the granting of the license, "as indicated by the applicant's intentions, plans, and ability to bring the invention to practical application or otherwise promote the invention's utilization by the public"; and (3) the agency must ensure that the scope of exclusivity is no greater than reasonably necessary to achieve these goals. Similarly, the exclusive licensee must commit "to achieve practical application of the invention within a reasonable time." Finally, the agency must ensure that "granting the license will not tend to substantially lessen competition or create or maintain a violation of the Federal antitrust laws." The agency is authorized to terminate the license if any of these provisions is violated.[5]

In sum, these provisions require each federal agency to ensure that the licensing of its inventions and related patents is accomplished in a manner that supports the public interest, recognizing the general principles discussed in the introduction to this chapter. Exclusive licenses are subject to particular scrutiny as they allow an agency to confer the benefits of a federal invention—developed at taxpayer expense—on a single licensee to the exclusion of all others. Thus, the agency must determine that the limitations on broad adoption of the invention that arise from an exclusive license are justified and serve the public interest, rather than merely the commercial interests of the licensee and the agency.

Some federal agencies have taken the position that granting an exclusive license to a fundamental technology can confer a substantial commercial advantage on a single licensee at the expense of the overall market and the advancement of science and technology. However, a recent article identifies cases in which federal agencies have granted exclusive licenses on federal inventions to patent assertion entities (PAEs) (Reilly and Waxman, 2016). This article reports that between 2006 and 2015, four federal agencies (the National Security Agency [NSA], NASA, the U.S. Navy, and the U.S. Air Force) granted exclusive or partially exclusive licenses covering more than 200 federal patents to seven different PAEs. As has been widely reported in the popular media, PAEs are extremely controversial to the extent that they extract monetary licensing fees or litigation settlements from existing market actors, and do not themselves innovate, utilize technology, or bring products to market. Reilly and Waxman (2016) report that during 2006–2015, in exchange for exclusive rights to federal inventions, the agencies received from the PAEs up-front payments, including at least one in excess of $2 million, as well as ongoing royalties. Further, the licensing activities

---

[5] 35 U.S.C. § 209(d)(3).

to PAEs do not appear to spur innovation (Feldman and Lemley, 2018). Although it is unclear how these exclusive licenses of federal technology served the public interest, promoted the dissemination and use of the patented inventions, or otherwise complied with the requirements of Section 209, courts have found that private parties cannot enforce the provisions of Section 209.[6]

There is no evidence that issuing licenses when the public interest is not served (such as licensing to PAEs) is a common occurrence, largely because no audit has been conducted to determine whether federal laboratories are issuing exclusive licenses that are in the public interest. Such an audit could be conducted by the Government Accountability Office (GAO) to determine the extent of the problem and continued on an ongoing basis to help provide information about future licensing. Such an audit would check to make sure that license agreements include strong downstream controls, such as licensing to others if the exclusive licensee is unable or unwilling to meet demand (Feldman et al., 2020).

While the public interest requirements regarding exclusive licenses apply to GOGO labs, Section 209 does not place similar requirements on government-owned, contractor-operated (GOCO) labs (although some agencies, such as DOE, have issued rules mimicking Section 209's public interest requirements). Although it is assumed that licensing will produce welfare gains by, among other things, promoting the introduction of new products to the market and the diffusion of technical knowledge, an explicit public interest requirement would allow the GOCO labs to consider alternative avenues for commercialization that could include firms, researchers, entrepreneurs, and inventors not usually invited into partnerships or collaboration with the labs.

Perhaps more important, there appears to be no effective remedy for violation of the Section 209 requirements on the part of federal agencies. Such remedies as recognition of such a violation as constituting an affirmative defense to a claim of infringement by an exclusive licensee of a federal patent or as giving rise to a private cause of action for the violation would help ensure that exclusive licensing by federal labs was in the public interest.

---

[6] For example, Reilly and Waxman (2016) describe an encryption technology patent that the Naval Research Laboratory (NRL) licensed exclusively to Network Signatures, Inc., a known PAE. During the 5 years following the granting of this license, Network Signatures initiated 89 patent infringement lawsuits against a range of businesses, including Wal-Mart, Harley Davidson, and Goldman Sachs. Most of the cases were settled for undisclosed amounts. When one defendant, Citibank, challenged Network Signatures' exclusive license from NRL as noncompliant with Section 209, the court held that the Bayh-Dole Act does not provide for a private cause of action and dismissed the claim (Network Signatures, Inc. v. Citibank, N.A., 2008 W.L. 5216032, at *3 [C.D. Cal. Dec. 4, 2008]). Rather, the only avenue for enforcing the provisions of Section 209 appears to be the agency's own administrative notice and comment process initiated prior to the granting of any such license (Southern Research Inst. v. Griffin Corp., 938 F.2d 1249, 1253 [11th Cir. 1991]). However, such an *ex ante* procedure requires vigilance and the expenditure of substantial resources by potential infringers of licensed patents.

Inventions Developed under a Cooperative Research and Development Agreement

Under the 1986 amendments to the Stevenson-Wydler Act, a federal laboratory that is a party to a CRADA may grant to its collaborating party an exclusive license to or assignment of any inventions made by employees of the lab. Federal labs that own inventions arising from a CRADA are subject to the restrictions concerning licensing of federal inventions that are enumerated in 35 U.S.C. § 209.

In contrast, no such restrictions constrain collaborators to whom rights of ownership over inventions have been granted *ex ante*, even if federal employees have contributed to those inventions. In principle, however, the lab retains the right to use, or have used, the invention for government purposes.[7] Likewise, CRADAs must allow for the collaborating party to retain title to any invention made by its employees, subject to the granting of a nonexclusive license permitting the lab to use, or have used, the invention for government purposes.[8] While no reporting requirements attach to patents on inventions owned by collaborating parties, the USPTO does require that the face of issued patents reflect the use of federal funding by contractors.

Other Federally Funded Inventions

Under the Bayh-Dole Act, entities that receive federal funding, including contractors of GOCO laboratories, are entitled to retain rights to inventions they make in the course of government-funded research.[9] These entities are free to license such rights, with the provision that any exclusive licensee must agree that products embodying, or produced using, the licensed invention will be manufactured substantially in the United States.[10] In contrast with the comparable U.S. manufacturing requirement applicable to federal inventions under 35 U.S.C. § 209, however, Section 204 authorizes the funding agency to waive this requirement if not commercially feasible.

Reporting on Patents by Federal Laboratories

Current reporting requirements, including patent reporting requirements, for federal laboratories are discussed in detail in Chapter 7. In that discussion, the committee reviews the significant empirical limitations associated with those

---

[7] 15 U.S.C. § 3710a(b)(1). Notwithstanding this statutory provision, the committee heard evidence that some contractors may nevertheless charge the agency for the use of this technology when an express acknowledgment of the government's retained rights is not set forth in the relevant contract.
[8] 15 U.S.C. § 3710a(b)(2).
[9] 35 U.S.C. § 204(a).
[10] 35 U.S.C. § 204. In addition, some agencies have issued directives on exclusive licensing that follow the concepts in Section 209 that apply to GOGO labs. See, e.g., DOE Order 483.1B, "DOE Cooperative Research and Development Agreements," December 12, 2016.

requirements and suggests mechanisms for addressing those limitations. This chapter focuses on one limitation on patent reporting that is specific to the current statutory structure, 15 U.S.C. § 3710(f), and associated regulatory guidance. Under the current NIST Guidance for Preparing Annual Technology Transfer Reports, federal labs are required to report annually on the patents they own and the number of CRADAs they have executed. However, there appears to be no mechanism for tracking patents, or any other innovation metric, associated with CRADAs. Given that both the academic literature and industry point to CRADAs as one of the most successful mechanisms for technology transfer and commercialization from the federal government (as discussed in Chapter 7 and other chapters), the absence of additional tracking with respect to CRADAs appears to be a deficiency of the current legal/guidance regime.

TRADE SECRETS

This section provides an overview of trade secret law and its intersection with the Freedom of Information Act (FOIA) for federal digital products.

Trade Secret Law

Trade secret law exists at both the state and federal levels in the United States. At the state level, almost all states have adopted some version of the Uniform Trade Secrets Act (UTSA) published by the Uniform Law Commission. At the federal level, the 2016 Defend Trade Secrets Act (DTSA), 18 U.S.C. § 1836 et seq., offers a similar civil cause of action.[11] Under each of these statutory regimes, the owner of a trade secret can bring an action against a party that obtains, uses, or discloses a trade secret without the owner's authorization.

As defined in Section 1.4 of the UTSA, a trade secret constitutes "information, including a formula, pattern, compilation, program, device, method, technique, or process, that: (i) derives independent economic value, actual or potential, from not being generally known to, and not being readily ascertainable by proper means by, other persons who can obtain economic value from its disclosure or use, and (ii) is the subject of efforts that are reasonable under the circumstances to maintain its secrecy." Under the DTSA, information that can constitute a trade secret comprises "all forms and types of financial, business, scientific, technical, economic, or engineering information, including patterns, plans, compilations, program devices, formulas, designs, prototypes, methods, techniques, processes, procedures, programs, or codes, whether tangible or intangible, and whether or how stored, compiled, or memorialized physically, electronically, graphically, photographically, or in writing," with the same secrecy and economic value requirements as those of the UTSA.[12] Trade secrets can

---

[11] In addition, the Economic Espionage Act of 1996, 18 U.S.C. § 1831 et seq., creates a federal criminal action for trade secret misappropriation.
[12] 18 U.S.C. § 1839(3).

include a range of confidential commercial and business information, such as customer and prospect lists, sales forecasts, marketing plans, manufacturing processes, ingredient lists, bills of material, component costs, proprietary algorithms, and the like. It is important to note, however, that trade secret law relates to *commercial* information and not to government classified information, which is administered and regulated under 32 C.F.R. Part 2001, "Classified National Security Information."

Trade secret protection lasts as long as the holder of the information makes reasonable efforts to maintain its confidentiality. Thus, a voluntary public disclosure of information by its holder, whether in a press release or a product manual, generally eliminates trade secret status. An exception is made if the information is disclosed to third parties pursuant to an enforceable nondisclosure or confidentiality agreement. Trade secrets also can be used without liability by third parties that use proper means, such as reverse engineering or independent invention, to acquire them. Because the contents of a U.S. patent application generally become public 18 months after filing, inventions disclosed in patent applications generally lose trade secret protection. For this reason, trade secret law is often described as an alternative to patents as a mode of protection (Lemley, 2011).

Many firms utilize trade secrets to protect digital products, particularly when other forms of legal protection, such as patent and copyright, are unavailable. Thus, commercial data and databases, which are not protected by copyright in the United States, are often treated as trade secrets, as are proprietary algorithms, particularly because patent protection for pure algorithms is unavailable.

Computer software may also be treated as a trade secret, even when copyright protection exists as well. For example, a firm may consider customized software it developed and uses internally (e.g., for economic modeling or programmed trading) to be a trade secret. The trade secret status of computer software that has been publicly distributed has vexed courts and commentators for decades (see Dratler, 1985; Katyal, 2020). For purposes of this discussion, suffice it to say that the combination of restrictive software licensing agreements that require users to maintain the confidentiality of even mass market software and the difficulty of extracting intelligible source code from executable object code programs has resulted in general recognition of trade secret protection for the internal mechanics of most publicly distributed software programs. That protection extends to their source code, though not necessarily to their visible screen displays or output (1 Milgrim on Trade Secrets § 1.09[5][b]). Needless to say, open-source code software, in which source code is made freely available to the public, is not subject to trade secret protection.

Commentators have criticized the increasing use of trade secrecy to protect digital products. Trade secrets do not require any disclosure, and legal protection is available for as long as secrecy is maintained (Thomas, 2014). Trade secrets may also stymie scientific disclosure and progress[13] because in contrast with the patent and copyright systems, which are designed to induce dissemination to the public, a trade secret's value lies in its secrecy, which forecloses public access to the knowledge. Additionally, using trade secrets may result in a loss of future innovative ability due to decreased labor mobility (Marx and Fleming, 2020) or decreased incentives for inventors (Contigiani and Hsu, 2019; Contigiani et al., 2018). In her econometric analysis, Williams (2013) concludes that the release of genomic data into the public domain by the HGP was associated with the generation of more commercial products relative to the release of genomic data kept as trade secrets (and licensed accordingly) by Celera, the HGP's major private competitor (Williams, 2013). As Professor Katherine Strandburg explained to the committee,[14] trade secret law is particularly problematic because it reduces the potential for others to build on existing innovations; it lacks certain moderating doctrines, such as fair use, that characterize copyright and, to a lesser extent, patent law; and it may compromise quality control, reproducibility, and accountability. According to Fromer (2019), moreover, technological advances suggest that one key moderating doctrine for trade secrets, the propriety of reverse engineering, may be less effective for digital products than for nondigital products because digital products are increasingly perceived as more difficult to reverse engineer as a result of developments in, among other things, cloud computing, machine learning, and automation.

Intersection of the Freedom of Information Act and Trade Secret Law for Federal Digital Products

FOIA[15] was enacted in 1966 to promote open government by ensuring that members of the public have access to federal agency records. It requires each federal agency (excluding Congress, courts, certain military authorities, and others) to make its records available promptly to any person that requests them, subject to reasonable procedures and fees.[16] Agency records, for purposes of FOIA, include both physical and electronic records.[17]

FOIA plays an important role in the dissemination and public use of federal digital products. Even though government works are free from copyright under Section 105(a) of the Copyright Act, there is no other assurance that federal laboratories will provide these works to the public. As one commentator notes, "the absence of copyright does not by itself make federal government information available for general use....In theory, the Copyright Act and the FOIA work together to ensure public availability and unrestricted use of government data. The

---

[13] Presentation to the committee by Brian Lally, DOE, December 5, 2019.
[14] Presentation to the committee by Prof. Katherine J. Strandburg, March 3, 2020.
[15] Pub. L. No. 89-487; 5 U.S.C. § 552.
[16] 5 U.S.C. § 552(a)(3)(A). But as noted by Reichman and Uhlir (2003), FOIA is itself an imperfect mechanism for accessing information, as the process is "time consuming and bureaucratic."
[17] 5 U.S.C. § 552(f)(2).

two laws are complementary parts of policy that supports public access to federal information resources."[18]

There are, however, numerous exceptions to FOIA disclosure requirements, including information that is classified, constitutes personnel or medical files, reflects agencies' internal deliberative processes, or pertains to law enforcement.[19] In addition, an agency is not required under FOIA to disclose privileged or confidential "trade secrets and commercial or financial information" that it has obtained from a nongovernmental third party.[20] Thus, if a private party submits trade secret information to a federal agency pursuant to an application or investigation, the agency ordinarily will not be allowed to release that information in response to a FOIA request. While the trade secret exception provides some benefits (e.g., enabling the filing of patent applications before information is released to the public), it has been criticized for both its breadth and its ambiguity (Levine, 2011). In addition, if information is created by a federal lab working with a private collaborator under a CRADA, then under the Stevenson-Wydler Act, that information may be treated as a trade secret and excluded from release under FOIA for a period of up to 5 years after its creation.[21]

There is some uncertainty as to whether computer software developed by or for a federal agency (not operating under a CRADA) constitutes an agency "record" subject to FOIA, and little statutory guidance addresses this issue. In the only reported case addressing this issue that the committee could identify, a Federal District Court distinguished between "generic word processing or prefabricated software," which does not constitute a "record" for purposes of FOIA, and software developed by an agency researcher in order to access and manipulate a particular database, which does constitute a "record" subject to FOIA (Cleary, Gottlieb, Steen & Hamilton v. Dept. Health & Human Services, 844 F. Supp. 770, 782 [D.D.C. 1993]). Today, the online *DOD Freedom of Information Act Handbook* (DOD, 2020) explains that "a record is the product(s) of data compilation, such as all books, papers, maps, and photographs, machine readable materials, inclusive of those in electronic form or format, or other documentary materials, regardless of physical form or characteristics," which appears to be less directed to software. Thus, software may or may not be within the scope of federal works accessible to the public under FOIA, at least in the view of DOD.

Trade Secret Status for Federal Digital Products

As early as the 1990s, critics of the federal government's open-access policies argued that FOIA has been an "impediment" to agencies' technology commercialization activities, given that "a foreign competitor can come in

---

[18] Gellman, 1994, p. 1004.
[19] 5 U.S.C. § 552(b).
[20] 5 U.S.C. § 552(b)(4).
[21] 15 U.S.C. § 3710a(c)(7)(B). This treatment appears to have been proposed in GAO, 1988 at 3.

through a FOIA and ask a Federal laboratory individual to give information on their research in progress, which was never the intent of FOIA" (U.S. House, 1992, p. 53 [Statement of Assistant Secretary of Commerce for Technology Policy Deborah Wince-Smith]; see also Chandler [1991, p. 404]: "Another significant obstacle frustrating the Government's ability to transfer computer software technology is the requirement of public disclosure pursuant to [FOIA]."). Thus, opposition to the release of government digital products under FOIA resonates with both the perceived need for exclusivity in federal technology transfer and the fear of foreign free riders.

In response, Section 801(b) of the 2013 National Defense Authorization Act, Pub. L. No. 113-66, was enacted to provide a special 5-year FOIA exemption for unclassified computer software and documentation developed at a DOD laboratory for military purposes.[22] This FOIA exemption applies if the software would have qualified as a trade secret had it been obtained from a private party, effectively putting DOD-developed software on par with software developed by a private party under a CRADA (discussed above). As a result, this unclassified government software can be withheld from parties making FOIA access requests absent any traditional exemption from FOIA. Section 801(b) also authorizes the DOD lab to license the trade secrets in this software to third parties if, among other things, the public is notified of the availability of the software and related documentation for licensing, and interested parties have a fair opportunity to submit licensing applications, the licenses comply with the requirements of 35 U.S.C. § 209, and the software was originally developed to meet DOD's military needs.[23] Such licenses may be exclusive or nonexclusive. The first reported license issued under this authority was granted by the Air Force Research Laboratory to Pratt & Whitney and United Technologies Corporation in 2018 on a nonexclusive basis.[24] Given the arguments raised above regarding the impact of trade secrets on innovation, it is clear that unless there is a national security issue, from a public interest perspective, trade secrets are a less desirable form of IP protection for federal labs' digital products.

---

[22] The provisions of Section 801 originally expired in 2017 but were extended through 2021 under Pub. L. No. 114-328, § 818. A representative of the Office of Naval Research told the committee that that agency hoped the provision would soon be made "permanent." Presentation to the Committee, John Karasek, Supervisory Intellectual Property Counsel, Office of Naval Research, March 2, 2020.

[23] As a condition for granting such licenses, the DOD lab must notify the public of the availability of such licenses and ensure that interested parties have a fair opportunity to submit applications for licensing. And if the DOD lab wishes to grant *exclusive* licenses to such software, it must comply with the public interest requirements under Section 209 of the Bayh-Dole Act.

[24] "AFRL signs first of its kind software license with Pratt & Whitney," Apr. 25, 2018, https://www.wpafb.af.mil/News/Article-Display/Article/1503043/afrl-signs-first-of-its-kind-softwa re-license-with-pratt-whitney/.

INTELLECTUAL PROPERTY SURROGATES: CONTRACTUAL AND TECHNOLOGICAL MEASURES

As discussed earlier in this chapter, many valuable digital products created by federal laboratories lack formal IP protection. As discussed in the next chapter, with a few conspicuous exceptions, copyright does not exist in government works. In addition, patents are difficult to obtain for digital inventions, and FOIA eliminates the less desirable trade secret protection for unclassified agency information. Nevertheless, federal agencies seeking to incentivize commercialization and/or extract rent from the transfer of these digital products to the private sector can circumvent this lack of protection via two distinct routes. First, as described earlier in this chapter, they can continue to obtain a range of statutory, regulatory, and judicial exceptions to the baseline legal exclusions from IP protection for these works. Second, by imposing restrictive contractual terms and technological control mechanisms on these digital products, they can compensate for the lack of legal protection. These mechanisms act as surrogates for IP protection.[25]

Commentators and courts have long recognized the power of contract and access mechanisms to limit the use of digital products even without express IP protection through private contracts. Thus, it is relatively settled law that software license agreements may prohibit users from taking such actions as reverse engineering that would otherwise be permissible fair use under U.S. copyright law (Bowers v. Baystate Techs., Inc., 320 F.3d 1317 [Fed. Cir. 2003]).

Over the years, federal agencies have taken advantage of a number of mechanisms—including nondisclosure agreements, license agreements, restrictions on redisclosure of information, and other types of controls—to exert greater control over federal digital products.[26] Such contractual limitations continue to be utilized today. Even without copyright, for example, the National Cancer Institute (NCI) distributes its NCIDOSE radiation dosimetry tools only in the form of executable object code and claims that "title in the Software shall remain with [NCI]." The software is released for noncommercial users under a free software transfer agreement that prohibits users from treating or diagnosing human subjects; using the software for commercial purposes; and copying, modifying, extending, or making derivatives of the software.[27] Parties interested in licensing the tools for commercial purposes must enter into a license agreement

---

[25] See Reichman and Uhlir, 2003, p. 381, "Electronic contracts become substitutes for intellectual property rights to the extent that they make it infeasible for third parties to obtain publicly disclosed but electronically fenced data without incurring contractual liability for damages."

[26] See Gellman (1994). The Digital Millennium Copyright Act (DMCA) of 1998, Pub. L. No. 105-304, 17 U.S.C. § 1201 et seq., prohibits the circumvention of any technological measure that protects a copyrighted digital work. The DMCA has often been cited as a significant legal barrier to the free use of public-domain data and other material (Reichman and Uhlir, 2003). Given the lack of copyright in government-created works, however, it is not clear that the DMCA is directly applicable to such works.

[27] See https://ncidose.cancer.gov/#agreement.

with NCI. These requirements appear designed to protect NCI from liability associated with use of the software.

FINDINGS AND RECOMMENDATIONS

Finding 4-1: Given documented cases in which federal laboratories have licensed software patents to patent assertion entities, it appears that federal labs do not always adhere to the requirements in Section 209 of the Bayh-Dole Act, which include allowing licensing only if such action is necessary to achieve practical application. However, evidence of how common such breaches are is limited. At the same time, there appears to be no effective remedy for violation of the Section 209 requirements on the part of federal agencies.

Finding 4-2: Exclusive software licenses are less valuable to the private sector if the software and source code are accessible via the Freedom of Information Act (FOIA). Using trade secrets to protect federal software, including source code, limits its accessibility to the public under FOIA.

Finding 4-3: Differences among federal agencies with respect to the trade secret exemption from the Freedom of Information Act appear to have no clear policy rationale.

Finding 4-4: Over the years, federal laboratories have taken advantage of a number of mechanisms—including nondisclosure agreements, license agreements, restrictions on redisclosure of information, and other types of controls—to extend their control over federal digital products, even in the absence of recognized intellectual property protection.

Recommendation 4-1: The Government Accountability Office or another appropriate, independent government entity should regularly, but not less than biennially, conduct a comprehensive assessment of the federal laboratories' compliance with public interest requirements in Section 209 of the Bayh-Dole Act related to issuance of exclusive patent licenses.

Recommendation 4-2: Congress should consider enacting mechanisms that provide greater legal force to public interest licensing requirements. For example, the violation of such requirements could be recognized as an affirmative defense to a claim of infringement by an exclusive licensee of a federal patent or give rise to a private cause of action for such violation.

Recommendation 4-3: Congress should consider imposing public interest licensing requirements on government-owned, contractor-operated laboratory contractors that are comparable to those imposed on their government-owned, government-operated counterparts under Section 209 of the Bayh-Dole Act.

Recommendation 4-4: Congress should consider rescinding the Section 801 authority provided by the 2008 National Defense Authorization Act that allows agencies to assert trade secrets even for unclassified information with no national security implication.

5

Copyrights, Digital Products, and Federal Laboratories

As described in the previous chapter, issues surrounding the government's ability to assert intellectual property rights in digital products, most notably software, are a key consideration in advancing their commercialization. Put differently, the ability of federal laboratories to control disposition of their digital products has a significant impact on the range of dissemination pathways available to the labs. For some digital outputs, such as data, the government's desire for broad dissemination has led to most government data's being freely available. For software, however, the government's ability to control its inventions and other inputs into innovation through patenting is more limited, particularly following the decision in Alice v. CLS Bank International 573 U.S. 208 (2014). Further, use of other mechanisms, such as trade secrets or restrictive contractual agreements, may inhibit innovation more broadly.

This chapter explores the potential role of copyright in advancing commercialization of digital products, especially software, created by federal labs. The discussion centers on a key consideration—that digital products created in government-owned, government-operated (GOGO) labs are excluded by Section 105 of the Copyright Act. This exclusion limits the labs' ability to disseminate and commercialize their digital products relative to government-owned, contractor-operated (GOCO) labs.

OVERVIEW OF COPYRIGHT IN DIGITAL PRODUCTS

The U.S. Copyright Act protects original works of authorship that are fixed in a tangible medium of expression, including digital copies (17 U.S.C. § 102[a]). These works include, among others, literary, pictorial, graphic, and audiovisual works. Literary works include all works "expressed in words, numbers, or other verbal or numerical symbols or indicia" (17 U.S.C. § 101). The following sections outline the degree to which certain digital products are generally copyrightable.

Data and Databases

Despite the expansive reach of the Copyright Act, it is well accepted under U.S. law that no copyright exists in facts, information, or data, as such. The Supreme Court reaffirmed this principle in Feist Publications v. Rural Telephone (499 U.S. 340 [1991]): "That there can be no valid copyright in facts is universally understood. The most fundamental axiom of copyright law is that no author may copyright his ideas or the facts he narrates." Under the principles set forth in *Feist*, the compiler of a collection of data may obtain a "thin" copyright in the creative arrangement and selection of entries in a database, but not in the data elements themselves, singly or in the aggregate.

By contrast, in 1996, the European Union adopted Directive 96/9 on the Legal Protection of Databases (the EU Database Directive), granting 15 years of legal protection to systematically arranged collections of data, information, or other material as long as it is accessible and its producer has made a substantial investment in its compilation (Reichman and Uhlir, 2003). Around the same time, a significant debate occurred in the United States regarding the advisability of enacting similar database protection legislation. Despite several competing proposals in Congress, no such legislation was enacted, leaving databases without formal legal protection in the United States (Reichman and Uhlir, 2003).

Nevertheless, commercial database compilers in the United States have largely compensated for this lack of legal protection by imposing restrictive contractual terms on those who access and use their databases. In some cases, these terms, coupled with technological impediments to access and use (the circumvention of which is prohibited by the Digital Millennium Copyright Act), may serve to limit the use of these data as much as or more than copyright.

Computer Software

The classic legal model of computer software contemplates two basic forms of computer code: *source code*—programming language instructions written (usually) by a human author; and *object code*—the machine-readable executable version of a source code program.[1] Given the clear analogy between the written programming language code of a software program and other written works of authorship (such as books and articles), computer software has long been considered a "literary work" for purposes of copyright protection (U.S. Copyright Office, 2017, § 721). This is the case even though lines of computer code are purely functional in nature, and copyright generally excludes the functional elements of a work (1 Nimmer on Copyright § 2A.10). By extension, the executable object code version of a computer program, which is manifested as a string of binary digits that is not comprehensible to most humans, is deemed to

---

[1] Though numerous hybrids and exceptions exist (e.g., pseudo code, interpreted code, etc.), this basic model is the foundation for the legal treatment of software. For a classic discussion of the distinction between object code and source code, see Dratler (1985, pp. 28–32).

constitute a different representation of that same copyrightable work and thus is also subject to copyright (U.S. Copyright Office, 2017, § 721.5), although this position was heavily contested at the outset (Samuelson, 1984; Miller, 1993). The protection of computer software under copyright law is now mandated under the Berne Convention for the Protection of Literary and Artistic Works (as amended on September 28, 1979) and the Agreement on Trade-Related Aspects of Intellectual Property Rights (TRIPS Agreement).

The degree to which aspects of a computer program beyond its written code instructions, such as its architecture and file structure, can be protected by copyright has also been subject to debate. Copyright protection extends only to the "expression" of an idea and not to "any idea, procedure, process, system, method of operation, concept, principle, or discovery" (17 U.S.C. § 102[b]), as such artifacts can be covered, if at all, by patents, trade secrets, and other forms of protection. Beginning in the 1980s, courts began to distinguish between protectable forms of software expression and unprotectable ideas regarding software architecture and structure (4 Nimmer on Copyright § 13.03[F]; Miller, 1993). Nevertheless, debate continues regarding the lines separating protectable and unprotectable software content, as suggested by the recent dispute in Oracle v. Google (cert. granted [2020]) over whether application programming interfaces (APIs) are copyrightable.

THE GOVERNMENT WORKS COPYRIGHT EXCLUSION

Most government publications, website content, audiovisual works, and other forms of content are copyright eligible in principle when fixed both in traditional (hard-copy, analog media) formats and in digital form. Nevertheless, Section 105(a) of the Copyright Act provides that "protection under this title is not available for any work of the United States Government...." A "work of the United States Government" is "a work prepared by an officer or employee of the United States Government as part of that person's official duties" (17 U.S.C. § 101). As described in the House Report accompanying the 1976 Copyright Act, "the effect of section 105 is intended to place all works of the United States Government, published or unpublished, in the public domain" (U.S. House, 1976, p. 59).

Despite the broad language of the government works exclusion, there are a number of exceptions. These exceptions, which permit the federal government to hold copyright in certain government works, are discussed below.[2]

---

[2] In addition to the exceptions discussed in this section, under the Postal Reorganization Act of 1970, Pub. L. No. 91-375, the U.S. Postal Service is permitted to obtain copyrights on the designs of postage stamps, stamped envelopes, souvenir cards, and other philatelic publications.

Standard Reference Data

In 1968, Congress enacted the Standard Reference Data Act, Pub. L. No. 90-396 (codified at 15 U.S.C. § 290), which recognized that "reliable standardized scientific and technical reference data are of vital importance to the progress of the Nation's science and technology." As a result, Congress sought, through the act, "to make critically evaluated reference data readily available to scientists, engineers, and the general public." To this end, it authorized and directed the secretary of commerce "to provide or arrange for the collection, compilation, critical evaluation, publication, and dissemination" of standardized scientific and engineering reference data (SRD).

To support the public dissemination of SRD, Congress expressly authorized the secretary of commerce or his/her designee to *sell* SRD provided that "to the extent practicable and appropriate, the prices established for such data may reflect the cost of collection, compilation, evaluation, and publication, and dissemination of the data, including administrative expenses" (15 U.S.C. § 290d). To eliminate any inconsistency between the new right to sell SRD and the government works exclusion in the Copyright Act noted above, the SRD Act created an express exception allowing the secretary to "secure copyright and renewal thereof on behalf of the United States as author or proprietor in all or any part of any standard reference data" notwithstanding any provisions of the Copyright Act to the contrary (15 U.S.C. § 290e).

The original impetus for the 1968 SRD Act may have arisen from concerns that foreign actors, particularly in Japan and the U.S.S.R., were using and reproducing valuable U.S. government data that had been made publicly available, and that legislation was needed to protect U.S. interests from this foreign competition.[3]

Today, the nation's SRD is administered by the National Institute of Standards and Technology (NIST), which states that it maintains 49 free and 14 fee-based SRD databases. These databases contain reference data and tools relevant to chemistry, engineering, materials science, computer science, physics, and other technical disciplines. The cost of fee-based SRD databases ranges from approximately $100 to $2,000, although the NIST website states that it does not accept purchase orders of less than $2,500.[4]

Changes to copyright law in the decades following the enactment of the SRD Act cast significant doubt on its continuing validity. The most important copyright development relevant to SRD was the Supreme Court's 1991 decision in *Feist*, in which the Court unambiguously rejected copyright protection for compilations of data. While the copyright status of data compilations may have been unclear in 1968 when the SRD Act was enacted, it was no longer ambiguous by 1991; compilations of data, including SRD, are not protected by copyright in

---

[3] See Nodiff, 1984, pp. 97–98 (discussing similar concerns arising from National Technical Information Services [NTIS] data).
[4] See https://www.nist.gov/srd/srd-catalog.

the United States. Nonetheless, the SRD Act, amended as recently as 2017, continues to give the secretary of commerce the power to obtain copyrights in SRD data. Thirty years after *Feist*, NIST's SRD may be the only unoriginal dataset in the United States that is protected by copyright. It also represents the first statutory exception to the exclusion of government works from copyright protection.

Transfers of Copyright to the Government

One exception to the government works exclusion occurs when ownership is transferred to the government from private sector entities. Although Section 105(a) of the U.S. Copyright Act generally precludes government copyright in its works, the Section nonetheless provides that "the United States Government is not precluded from receiving and holding copyrights transferred to it by assignment, bequest, or otherwise." Such transfers are rare, but do occur. For example, in connection with the development of the Ada computer programming language for the Department of Defense (DOD) from the 1970s through 1990s, DOD commissioned and subsequently obtained copyright in a number of explanatory documents from the Illinois Institute of Technology Research Institute (IITRI), which operated DOD's Ada Joint Program Office (IITRI, 1994). Some government-operated federal laboratories may use this mechanism to circumvent the copyright exclusion of Section 105(a). As one 2011 report notes, "Some GOGO laboratories have found creative ways to assert copyright protection. For example, one laboratory…employee explained that the laboratory obtains copyrights for software by asking the industry partner to assert the rights to the intellectual property, and then assign those rights to the laboratory" (Hughes et al., 2011, p. 53). Circumvention of the government works exclusion in this manner is expressly discouraged by the House Report on the 1976 Copyright Act.[5]

Foreign Copyright in U.S. Government Works

As noted above, Section 105(a) of the Copyright Act provides that "copyright protection *under this title* is not available for any work of the United States Government" (emphasis added). Some federal agencies have interpreted the exclusion under Section 105(a) to mean that the exclusion should apply only to the U.S. copyright that may inhere in government works, but not to foreign copyrights that may arise with respect to those same works. The Senate report accompanying the adoption of the 1976 Copyright Act makes this intention clear:

---

[5] "It can be assumed that, where a Government agency commissions a work for its own use merely as an alternative to having one of its own employees prepare the work, the right to secure a private copyright would be withheld" (U.S. House 1976, p. 59). Professor Nimmer appears to agree: "Could the U.S. Government thus claim a copyright in a work by this indirect method which it would be precluded from claiming if the work were in the first instance made in a for hire relationship? It seems unlikely that the courts would permit such a subterfuge" (1 Nimmer on Copyright § 5.06[B][3]).

> The prohibition on copyright protection for United States Government works is not intended to have any effect on protection of these works abroad. Works of the governments of most other countries are copyrighted, and there are no valid policy reasons for denying such protection to United States Government works abroad. (U.S. Senate, 1975, p. 56)

Nonetheless, it is not clear that Section 105(a), as a matter of U.S., foreign, or international law, actually does empower a U.S. government agency to hold a foreign copyright in a government work. The existence of such a foreign copyright is, of course, a question not of U.S. law but of the law of the foreign jurisdiction in question, as it is informed by the Berne Convention and other relevant international agreements. It is beyond the scope of this report to review the copyright laws of the 177 other signatory states to the Berne Convention, not to mention those of the handful of nonsignatory states. Yet some relevant observations can be made on the basis of the text of the Convention itself, as well as its application under U.S. law.

For example, while the Convention addresses the *types* of works that must be protected under the national copyright laws of every member state, it does not explicitly address *ownership* of those works. Ownership of a copyright is a matter of national law. And when an entity wishes to enforce a copyright in a country other than that in which the copyright originated, traditional conflict-of-laws rules must be applied. While those rules may vary from country to country, the application of U.S. conflict rules to questions of international copyright ownership is clear. In Itar-Tass Russian News Agency v. Russian Kurier, Inc., 153 F.3d 82 (2d Cir. 1998), the leading U.S case on this issue, the court determined that under applicable conflict rules, the law of the country of origin, rather than U.S. law, should govern questions of copyright ownership.

Accordingly, foreign courts considering whether to recognize copyright in a U.S. government work would most likely apply U.S. copyright ownership principles. For example, a court in France or Japan assessing whether to permit a U.S. government agency to enforce a French or Japanese copyright in a U.S. government work should look to U.S. law, and the exclusion from copyright under Section 105(a), to determine whether the U.S. agency holds a corresponding national copyright in that country, notwithstanding the lack of a U.S. copyright. Assuming that those countries observe conflict-of-laws principles comparable to those observed by the Second Circuit in *Itar-Tass*, the answer would likely be "no." Accordingly, a serious question exists regarding the position that U.S. federal agencies can hold foreign copyrights in U.S. government works as to which U.S. copyright is precluded under Section 105(a). The committee heard of assertions by federal laboratories of copyright ownership of software and other qualifying digital products founded principally on arguments regarding foreign copyrightability.[6] In the committee's view, however, such arguments suggest that

---

[6] Presentation to the committee by Jordan Kasper, Defense Digital Service, December 5, 2019.

federal labs are trying to avoid the consequences of Section 105(a) and the limits on their ability to use copyright to achieve public interest outcomes.

Civilian Faculty at Military Academic Institutions

The National Defense Authorization Act for Fiscal Year 2020 (Pub. L. No. 116-92) created an additional exception to the copyright exclusion for civilian faculty at any of 12 enumerated U.S. military academic institutions. Under Sections 105(b)–(c) of the Copyright Act (added by amendment in Pub. L. No. 116-92), the copyright in a scholarly work created by a civilian faculty member at those institutions is owned by the author, subject to a royalty-free copyright license for government use. This provision puts these faculty on a more even footing with faculty from universities and scientists in GOCO labs with respect to their research output.

Copyright and Government Contractors

Finally, the government works copyright exclusion applies only to officers and employees of the U.S. government. Therefore, it does not apply to works prepared for the government by contractors who are not government employees or by researchers who receive government funding.[7] Thus if a federal laboratory hires an external contractor to create a literary work or design a file for use by a federal laboratory, it will be subject to copyright *owned by the contractor*. Likewise, if a federal researcher collaborates with a contractor to create a joint work, such as software development, the contractor alone will hold copyright in that work, and neither the federal researcher, the lab, nor the governing federal agency will have any rights in it. However, government labs that are contractor-operated are eligible to own copyright in their works.

The omission of government contractors from the scope of the government works exclusion was clearly intentional. The Senate and House reports accompanying the adoption of the 1976 act explain that "the bill deliberately avoids making any sort of outright, unqualified prohibition against copyright in works prepared under Government contract or grant" (U.S. Senate, 1975, p. 56). Thus, while Congress acknowledged that "there may well be cases where it would be in the public interest to deny copyright in the writings generated by Government research contracts and the like," it also reasoned that "there are almost certainly many other cases where the denial of copyright protection would be unfair or would hamper the production and publication of important works" (id.). The Senate and House reports recommend that a balance between openness and copyright be struck on a case-by-case basis: "Where, under the particular circumstances, Congress or the agency involved finds that the need to have a work

---

[7] In 2003, Representative Martin Sabo (D-MN) introduced the Public Access to Science Act (H.R. 2613), which would have disallowed copyright protection for scientific work substantially funded by the U.S. government. The bill died in committee (see Contreras, 2013, p. 524).

freely available outweighs the need of the private author to secure copyright, the problem can be dealt with by specific legislation, agency regulations, or contractual restrictions" (id.).

The committee heard testimony that the ability of GOCO labs to own copyright in software is considered advantageous by lab and agency personnel. Robert Leland of the National Renewable Energy Laboratory (NREL) outlined the range of options for dissemination of software, with some specific examples, from his experience with NREL and Sandia National Laboratories, noting that having a variety of mechanisms available is useful in finding the mechanism that best maximizes diffusion and encourages productive partnerships with private firms.[8] The Department of Energy's (DOE's) Brian Lally noted that flexibility is a real challenge for government-operated labs because they lack copyright, telling the committee, "Particularly with software, maybe more than any other area, it is a real challenge for government-operated laboratories like NETL [the National Energy Technology Laboratory] or other federal labs at other agencies because if the software was developed by a federal employee, it is generally not copyrightable, at least not under current law."[9]

There is evidence that at least some federal agencies impose controls on their contractors' ability to assert copyright in works created at GOCO labs. For example, DOE's contract with Iowa State University for operation of the Ames Laboratory provides that the contractor may assert copyright in any given item of data or software only if it "can show that commercialization would be enhanced by such copyright protection."[10] Likewise, the National Aeronautics and Space Administration (NASA) Federal Acquisition Regulation (FAR) Supplement 1852.227-14(4)(i) (which applies to cooperative research and development agreements [CRADAs]) requires that the collaborator agree "not to assert claim to copyright, publish or release to others any computer software first produced in the performance of this contract unless the Contracting Officer authorizes through a contract modification." And according to information provided to the committee, "NASA rarely allows contractors to assert copyright" under this provision.[11]

APPLYING COPYRIGHT TO FEDERALLY CREATED SOFTWARE

Since the mid-1980s, proposals have been made to permit government-operated federal laboratories to obtain and hold copyright in the computer software they develop. This section first summarizes the history of these

---

[8] Presentation to the Committee, Robert Leland, National Renewable Energy Laboratory, December 5, 2019.
[9] Presentation to the Committee, Brian Lally, Department of Energy, December 5, 2019.
[10] Clause I.132(e) - DEAR 970.5227-2 Rights In Data-Technology Transfer (DEC 2000) (Deviation) (Jul 2006).
[11] Presentation to the Committee, Bryan Geurts, Chief Patent Counsel, NASA Goddard Space Flight Center, March 2, 2020 (Slides 5 and 7).

legislative and regulatory efforts and then assesses the arguments for federal software copyrights in light of the evidence gathered by the committee.

History of Efforts to Copyright Federal Software

In 1988 and 1990, the General Accounting Office (GAO),[12] at the request of two different congressional committees, interviewed officials at prominent federal laboratories and agencies[13] regarding their ability to transfer federally developed software to the private sector (GAO, 1988, 1990). These federal officials reported that "making software generally available allows for the adequate dissemination of most of their agencies' software" (GAO, 1991, p. 3).

One official at DOE indicated that most of the software distributed by the National Energy Software Center had "little commercial value" (GAO, 1988, p. 13). However, with respect to federally developed software that was believed to have commercial potential (about 10 percent of the total),[14] officials felt "constrained" by the lack of copyright protection and the requirement for public dissemination (GAO, 1988, p. 2; 1991, p. 3).

Between 1990 and 1992, Representative Constance Morella (R-MD) introduced three successive House bills seeking to award federal agencies copyright in software that they developed under CRADAs (copyright in software developed by private collaborators under a CRADA already being secured).[15] Each of these legislative proposals died in committee. More than three decades later, federal agencies are still seeking copyright protection for federally created software, most recently in the 2019 NIST Green Paper (NIST, 2019b, pp. 40–41) and in a recent set of proposals submitted to Congress.[16] The principal rationale advanced in support of these proposals is that the inability of the government to copyright software may slow or inhibit commercial development by the U.S. private sector (NIST, 2019b).

---

[12] Renamed the Government Accountability Office in 2004.
[13] The agencies interviewed for the GAO study included the Departments of Agriculture, Commerce, and Defense; the Environmental Protection Agency; the National Aeronautics and Space Administration; and the National Institutes of Health.
[14] This estimate is consistent with software commercialization figures reported by research universities, which are typically funded by federal grants but are permitted to obtain copyright in their software inventions. Specifically, as reported by the National Academies in 2011, software accounted for about 10 percent of both licensing activity and invention disclosures at research universities (NRC, 2011).
[15] See, e.g., Technology Transfer Improvements Act of 1990, 101st Cong., H.R. 5850; Technology Transfer Improvements Act of 1991, 102nd Cong., H.R. 191 and S. 1581; Technology Transfer Improvements Act of 1993, 103rd Cong., H.R. 523.
[16] National Institute of Standards and Technology, ROI Initiative Status Update: Legislative Package Sent to Congress, press release, December 10, 2020. See https://www.nist.gov/news-events/news/2020/12/roi-initiative-status-update-legislative-package-sent-congress.

The Committee's Consideration of Copyright for Federally Created Software

This chapter has described a number of exceptions to the government works copyright exclusion, most notably a recent one allowing access to copyright for faculty at certain federal military academic institutions. Making an additional, limited exception to allow copyright of software produced at GOGO laboratories would not be extraordinary. In making its overall assessment of this issue, the committee took into account a number of factors, described below.

The Exclusivity Incentive

The prevailing view among supporters of federal software copyright is that under certain circumstances, a private firm may be unwilling to make substantial investments in commercializing such software unless it can obtain exclusive rights to the underlying government code. Without this exclusivity, the firm's competitors could utilize the same code to create their own commercial offerings, thus reducing the return to the first firm. Because every firm would face the same potential competitive pressure, none might have the incentive to make the necessary up-front investment in adapting the government code to the commercial market.

Those who oppose copyright protection in government-created software argue that a grant of exclusivity would disregard the creative contribution that the private sector must make to that software in order to bring it to market.[17] Private firms can copyright their additions to or derivatives of public-domain software (U.S. House 1992, p. 158) (more specifically, "the derivative works provisions of the Copyright Act provide an excellent and adequate means for industry to protect work which they further develop that is based on or 'derived from' public domain government works" [written comments by the Software Publishers Association]). Thus, private firms are well equipped, technically and legally, to build differentiating features and functionality onto government-created software to compete in the marketplace.[18] One example from the 1980s is the Relational Information Manager (RIM) system developed for NASA by Boeing. A former NASA employee modified the publicly available RIM system for commercial settings and used it as the basis for a new line of database management products known as R:BASE, which became some of the best-selling database management products in the world.[19] However, the government's ability to commercialize such

---

[17] See U.S. House, 1992, pp. 31–32: "By some estimates, 90% of the effort in developing commercial software goes into the last 10% of the development and documentation effort. That in part explains why relatively little federal software ever reaches federal software distribution centers, such as NTIS: the agencies have little need or incentive to undertake the work necessary to meet distribution center standards."

[18] See presentation to the committee by Michael W. Carroll of the American University College of Law (March 2, 2020).

[19] See https://ntrs.nasa.gov/archive/nasa/casi.ntrs.nasa.gov/20020086972.pdf.

new additions, or to ensure that subsequent inputs by private firms benefit the public more broadly, can also be constrained by the federal lab's lack of copyright in the underlying work (Okediji, 2016).

Critics of copyright in federally created software also argue that the exclusion makes the software accessible at no cost to *all* commercial firms that wish to build upon it, not just the one(s) that has (have) entered into an agreement with a federal lab. The software thus becomes an input to commercial development at multiple companies, all free of charge. Governmental data and technology that have been made freely available in this manner—the GPS signal, the Internet, RIM, and the human genome—have resulted in major businesses and entirely new markets that have yielded substantial economic benefit. Because improvements are copyrightable, if the perceived return on investment is great enough, an investor will likely possess sufficient incentive to move forward.[20]

However, free software does not necessarily make available the kinds of software that produce either short- or long-term private and public benefits. Much software delivers its biggest impact only when it has been refined and adapted to the needs of downstream commercialization, a process that requires both capital and technological inputs. While reliance on free access to upstream software has developmental effects, undercapitalization of potentially valuable downstream applications may also occur when resources in the public domain are difficult or costly to find. Because of differences across individuals and companies with respect to resources, abilities, and opportunities, moreover, the benefits of information deposited in a public domain may accrue to just a few. For example, about half of the downloads from GenBank come from .com domains (Chander and Sunder, 2004).

Therefore, as described in Chapter 3 and in this chapter, the ability of federal labs to grant exclusive rights may be necessary for a diversity of private actors to make the additional investment required to commercialize federally produced software, although additional data may be needed in order to make a final determination on this question. The use of exclusive licenses may also be justified in circumstances where the commercialization of software developed by the government has broader societal benefits relative to the returns that could be captured by the private sector. Because software development cycles are relatively short, it would be advisable for such exclusive licenses to be of limited duration.

Absent copyright, the government's ability to issue licenses on government-created software is extremely limited. With copyright, the government might be able to include in its licensing agreements a number of downstream controls that would ensure that the licenses are in the public interest, similar to what has been suggested for contracts made by extramural awardees to ensure that taxpayer-funded innovations are in the public interest (Feldman et al., 2020). Such provisions in the government's licensing agreements might include (1) providing that the government can license to others if the exclusive licensee is

---

[20] See presentation to the committee by Michael W. Carroll of the American University College of Law (March 2, 2020).

unable or unwilling to meet demand, such as in times of shortage; (2) ensuring transparency of product or pricing information to the public; (3) disfavoring such behaviors as evergreening the invention with minor modification patents; and (4) providing that the technology must be used for creating a product or service rather than for monetization through a nonpracticing entity (Feldman et al., 2020). Moreover, the government might want to control digital products involving artificial intelligence to ensure transparency and verification of the underlying technology (Feldman, 2018).

Effects of Differential Treatment of GOGOs and GOCOs

As described in this chapter, the committee heard testimony that the lack of copyright is a constraint on government-operated laboratories, and that having copyright increases the range of options available to contractor-operated labs when determining the most effective way to disseminate the software they develop. As described in Chapter 4 on patents, there is evidence of increasing use of trade secrets and intellectual property surrogates to provide copyright-like protection. Without copyright, GOGO labs resort to restrictive contractual terms and technological control mechanisms to close the gap created by the lack of legal protection. As discussed in Chapter 4, these mechanisms impede scientific progress and innovation and may generate other negative externalities. These considerations suggest the need for a more rational overall approach to downstream applications of government-generated digital products. Moreover, the use of these backdoor methods is unevenly distributed and not fully understood across the federal labs, with the result that while some digital products are transferred downstream in imaginative ways, others are not.

Foreign Free Riders

Historically, one issue motivating the push to make copyright available for federal software has been concern over international competitiveness. One of the stated goals of the Stevenson-Wydler Act was "to improve the economic, environmental, and social well-being of the United States" (15 U.S.C. § 3702). As noted by GAO in its 1988 interviews, publicly disseminating unclassified scientific and technical information "does not distinguish between U.S. and foreign businesses" (GAO, 1988, p. 13). As a result, several federal agency officials believed that "foreign competitors" should not have equal access to U.S. technology through public dissemination (id.).

The "foreign free rider" problem—giving foreign firms free access to digital products developed at U.S. taxpayer expense—presents a challenge to models of open access and science. Its potential has been observed not only in the context of federally developed software but also in open-access publishing requirements for federally funded research (Contreras, 2013, pp. 539–540), the international use of inventions patented under the Bayh-Dole Act (Hemel and

Ouellette, 2017, pp. 3–4), and the sharing of government-generated data (Reichman and Uhlir, 2003, pp. 423–425).

Nevertheless, it remains unclear that giving foreign firms free access to digital products produced by federal labs is necessarily detrimental to U.S. businesses or consumers. First, in today's globalized market, it is difficult to know what firms are "domestic" versus "foreign." Most large firms, particularly in the technology sector, have operations in multiple countries, and their headquarters, manufacturing facilities, and research and development (R&D) operations are often located on the basis of favorable tax treatment, labor costs, and proximity to supply chains rather than notions of national identity. Moreover, consumers often benefit from global competition among suppliers, even as local suppliers give way to more efficient, low-cost, and innovative foreign competitors.

One solution to the foreign free rider problem would be to enable U.S. federal laboratories that are government-operated to obtain copyright in their software (as is the case in many countries for government-funded works), so that the laboratories could control the subsequent distribution of federal software (and presumably ensure that only U.S. firms were authorized to commercialize it) (Chandler, 1991, p. 406). Others have proposed diplomatic solutions in which other nations would be urged to adopt policies of openness akin to those of the United States (Reichman and Uhlir, 2003, p. 425).

Over the years, federal labs have tested more incremental approaches. As reported by GAO, "the National Energy Software Center does not announce the availability of new software to foreign organizations for 2 years after it is announced to U.S. organizations" (GAO, 1988, p. 13). GAO also noted that NASA made only executable object code versions of its software (and not source code) available to foreign entities (id. at n.6). It is not clear how effective these measures have been in conferring the benefits of this federally developed software primarily on U.S. entities, but it appears that none of these agencies currently discriminate against non-U.S. entities in terms of software distribution. Nonetheless, no downstream controls can be placed on users of government-created digital products without the government's having copyright.

Copyright Considerations for Open-Source Software Licensing

Many of the arguments made in the late 1980s and early 1990s regarding copyright in federally developed software were predicated on an entirely different software development and distribution environment from that of today. The open-source software (OSS) movement emerged in 1989 with the release of the GNU General Public License, but did not attract significant attention until the popularization of the Linux operating system in the mid-1990s and the 1997 publication of Eric Raymond's seminal article "The Cathedral and the Bazaar" (Raymond, 1999). Today, OSS dominates many market segments. The OSS Android operating system runs on more than 86 percent of all smartphones in the world; in 2019 IBM paid $34 billion for Red Hat, the distributor of Linux software packages; and Microsoft owns and operates GitHub, a platform and user community that hosts thousands of OSS projects, which it acquired in 2018 for $7.5 billion.

The use of OSS today is a viable commercial model that pervades nearly every segment of the economy. And while the integration of OSS into commercial software products, particularly under copyleft and similar forms of OSS licenses, can be challenging, most software-based businesses have adopted policies and practices that enable the integration of OSS and proprietary software in an effective and legally sound manner. In short, the existence of copyright does not impede recourse to OSS and may actually facilitate it when properly employed in that context.

Commitments to the Public Domain

Another way that federal laboratories distribute software and other digital products on an open basis is through contributions to the public domain.[21] In its Open Source Software FAQ, DOD states, "You must release it as 'public domain' (when releasing it at all) if it was developed by a U.S. government employee as part of their official duties."[22]

While one might argue that under Section 105(a) of the Copyright Act, software developed by federal employees is already in the public domain, documentation evidencing the contribution of software to a larger OSS project is often needed. One legal mechanism for making such a contribution is the Creative Commons (CC) "no rights reserved" commitment to the public domain ("CC0"). To make a CC0 contribution, a software developer must simply apply the "CC0" mark to the work and indicate that it is contributed to the public domain under the CC0 terms, which are set forth in full on the CC website.[23] Another mechanism for contributing a work to the public domain is the Zero-Clause BSD/Free Public License 1.0.0 (0BSD),[24] an ultrashort license that states, "Permission to use, copy, modify, and/or distribute this software for any purpose with or without fee is hereby granted," followed by a comprehensive disclaimer of liability.

Software placed in the public domain can easily be integrated into and used in combination with proprietary or OSS software, as it carries no restrictions of its own regarding use or distribution. If a subsequent, downstream user incorporates public-domain software into a larger software program and releases it under an OSS or proprietary software license, any copyright-based restrictions on use of that public-domain software will not be enforceable, just as the copyright in a legal textbook would have no effect on the text of the U.S. Constitution quoted therein.

While commitments to the public domain are the simplest mechanisms for publicly distributing government software, the contributor retains no right to

---

[21] There is no statutory mechanism in the United States or most other countries for contributing a copyrighted work to the public domain (Fagundes and Perzanowski, 2020).
[22] See https://dodcio.defense.gov/Open-Source-Software-FAQ/.
[23] See https://creativecommons.org/publicdomain/zero/1.0/legalcode.
[24] See https://opensource.org/licenses/0BSD.

control the use of the software, even under contract. Thus, a lab that wishes to contribute software to the public while imposing at least some conditions for the public interest may need to utilize a customized agreement or a modified OSS agreement that includes some contractual commitments and conditions (e.g., attribution of the originating lab, user registration, or a commitment to make any modifications or derivatives publicly available (known as share-alike or copyleft terms)).

Federal Distribution of Open-Source Software without Copyright

Pursuant to the Federal Source Code Policy and their own internal policies, a number of federal laboratories—both GOGO and GOCO—have released source code under permissive OSS licenses, such as the Apache, BSD, Eclipse, and MIT licenses.[25] As noted earlier, however, most OSS licenses are copyright licenses. Because federal labs lack copyright in software products they independently develop (i.e., not at a GOCO lab or in conjunction with private parties to a CRADA), the legal basis for these labs to release software under one of the common OSS license agreements remains unclear. This section reviews legal mechanisms that have emerged over the years to enable the "licensing" of works created by federal employees and agencies.

Agreements relating to the distribution of OSS developed by federal employees must rely for enforcement on contract law rather than copyright (NASEM, 2018, p. 23). While this approach is effective for many purposes, it is not without drawbacks. For example, OSS license commitments could be deemed by a court to constitute conditions to the copyright license rather than contractual obligations. Accordingly, if a licensee violated these commitments, the plaintiff copyright owner would be entitled to the full range of copyright infringement damages, potentially including statutory damages. Had the violation simply been a breach of contract, contractual expectation damages would likely have been more modest. In a government software agreement, contractual commitments can be imposed on the user, but without a copyright on the underlying software, remedies for copyright infringement will not be available.

In addition, the existence of copyright enables the copyright owner to police the use of its software beyond the original licensee with which it entered into an agreement. That is, if the licensee of a software component breaches its agreement, then even without copyright, the licensor may bring a claim for breach of contract. But if the licensee distributes the software to others who distribute it still further, the original licensor lacks contractual privity with those downstream users and generally will be unable to bring a contractual claim against them. If the licensor had copyright in the software, it could bring copyright infringement claims against those unauthorized downstream users.

The absence of copyright in federal software places a federal licensor in a somewhat weaker position relative to similarly situated commercial licensor,

---

[25] Information provided in various presentations to the committee.

but this does not necessarily argue against the distribution of federal software using OSS-like agreements. Rather, it may suggest the need to adjust the underlying rules to better align the government's interest in dissemination of federally created software with commercialization opportunities.

NASA has been particularly engaged in the development of government-appropriate software agreements that are not grounded in the ownership of copyright. In 2003, NASA developed a customized OSS license (the NASA Open Source Agreement or NOSA) expressly acknowledging that no copyright existed in software developed solely by government employees (see NASEM, 2018, p. 23–25). NOSA v. 1.3[26] was approved by the Open Source Initiative (OSI) in 2004 as compliant with the Open Source Definition.[27] Shortly thereafter, however, the Free Software Foundation found fault with one of the clauses of the NOSA v. 1.3 license and declared that it was "not a free software license" at all (FSF, 2020).[28] In response to this critique, NASA developed a new version of NOSA (v. 2.0) and submitted it to OSI for approval around 2013 (NASEM, 2018, p. 25). As of this writing, however, NOSA v. 2.0 has still not been approved.

Following the NOSA controversy, observers both within and outside of NASA called on the agency to release NASA-developed software "under whatever mainstream open source license makes sense within the development environment it is being released within" (Beyer et al., 2018). Such calls are well intentioned, but appear to miss the point that "normal" copyright-based OSS licenses are not appropriate for the dissemination of software that lacks copyright because it is developed by federal employees. NASA may have reached an acceptable compromise with respect to its Nebula software, which it contributed to the Open Stack Project in 2012 using what has been termed a modified version of the Apache software contributor's license that was tailored for public-domain contributions.

Other federal agencies have also come to appreciate the need for customized or noncopyright licenses when distributing software and other digital products. For example, the National Cancer Institute distributes its NCIDOSE radiation dosimetry tools under a software transfer agreement that contains numerous contractual restrictions, but carefully avoids any mention of copyright.

The lack of copyright in federal software has clearly introduced complexity with regard to the release of such software on an OSS basis. While some labs, as discussed above, have developed agreements that attempt to mirror traditional OSS licenses, most have not. Labs that have most effectively

---

[26] See https://opensource.org/licenses/NASA-1.3.
[27] See https://opensource.org/docs/osd.
[28] Clause 3.G of NOSA 1.3 provides, "Each Contributor represents that that its Modification is believed to be Contributor's original creation and does not violate any existing agreements, regulations, statutes or rules, and further that Contributor has sufficient rights to grant the rights conveyed by this Agreement." According to the Free Software Foundation, this requirement limits modifications to contributor-developed code (original creations) and precludes the use of third-party code in modifications. "Free software development depends on combining code from third parties, and the NASA license doesn't permit this" (FSF, 2000).

distributed software under one of these customized agreements comply with the law, but these agreements are unfamiliar to most of the OSS community. Labs that rely instead on traditional OSS license agreements (e.g., Apache, BSD, or GPL) fit more easily within existing OSS projects, but misrepresent the nature of rights they hold in federal software. This situation could be rationalized if federal labs held copyright in their software. Adding copyright to the already available option of patent protection for federally created software would provide the federal labs with discretion to determine which of the two regimes would best facilitate commercialization and the public interest in any given case.

LIMITING AND ASSESSING COPYRIGHT AND EXCLUSIVE LICENSING OF SOFTWARE DEVELOPED BY GOGO FEDERAL LABORATORIES

If Congress should decide to allow copyright protection in government-created software, it would nonetheless be necessary to place certain limitations on federal agencies' abilities to grant exclusive software licenses. Doing so would be consistent with the spirit of Section 209 of the Bayh Dole Act of 1980 (35 U.S. § 209), which limits a federal agency to granting exclusive or partially exclusive licenses only when exclusivity is necessary to induce follow-on development, as discussed further in Chapter 4 on patents. Such limits on federal agencies' abilities to grant exclusive software licenses would need to include, among others, limits on their duration and consideration of what was needed to bring the software to practical application or to promote the software's utilization for the public benefit. Moreover, similar to the public notice requirement in Section 209 of the Bayh-Dole Act, any agency providing exclusive software copyright licenses would be required to publish such licenses in the *Federal Register*. Finally, within 5 years of the enactment of a provision allowing copyright in government-created software, it would be advisable for NIST to commission a study to determine the effects of the provision on the use, dissemination, and commercialization of federally developed software.

ADVANCING COHERENCE IN GOVERNMENT SOFTWARE POLICY

When the 1976 Copyright Act was devised and enacted, considerable thought was given to making the new act hospitable to computer programs. However, those exercises did not focus on the potential need to deal with government-generated computer programs under the general waiver of Section 105(a) for "government works." There are now good reasons to believe that amending Section 105(a) to exclude computer software (resulting in government ownership of its own software) might simplify addressing the problems described in this chapter. The current preference for free riding on tax-funded government-generated software is hardly persuasive. What is persuasive is the possibility that having copyright can enable the government to better control the uses of its own software for both public and private purposes. Any public interest uses dependent on nongovernment ownership could be managed by direct waivers of the government copyright as needed.

At the same time, government copyright in software would greatly simply and facilitate the government's overall efforts to regulate this area comprehensively and consistently. In this respect, adding a government copyright to software would merely correct a historical anomaly introduced when the carveouts to Section 105(a) were first conceived and debated. All that was conceived and debated with regard to Section 105(a) at that time would remain untouched by the proposal to exclude government-generated software from its ambit. Indeed, the ability to hold copyright in government software might promote commercialization either by facilitating exclusive licensing, when needed, or by facilitating OSS licensing.

Finally, a number of exceptions to the government works exclusion rule already exist—notably the allowance for works prepared for the government by contractors, which means that GOCO and GOGO federal laboratories operate under different rules. Efforts by some GOGO labs to circumvent this restriction are, in some cases, unsound, and may result in suboptimal commercial outcomes. In sum, the government's policy making with regard to the software it generates would become more rational and coherent if it were based on an initial assumption of copyright ownership. Such ownership could, of course, be waived, freely licensed, or negated in its entirety as necessary to advance commercialization and promote the public interest. Thus allowing copyright protection for federally created software would strengthen the range of options available to government-operated labs to both commercialize the software they generate and enhance its use for the public good.

FINDINGS AND RECOMMENDATIONS

Finding 5-1: With some exceptions, the Copyright Act prohibits copyright in federally created works, and the federal government maintains a general policy of making such works accessible in a manner consistent with the public interest.

Finding 5-2: The inability of government-owned, government-operated laboratories to assert copyright in federally developed software creates incentives for those labs to circumvent existing rules in order to facilitate technology transfer and commercialization.

Finding 5-3: The statutory authorization of standard reference data (SRD) copyright has little legal justification. Moreover, there appears to be no economic rationale for retaining copyright in SRD because the National Institute of Standards and Technology, the current custodian and developer of SRD, makes 80 percent of SRD available free of charge without copyright and earns an insignificant amount from the remaining SRD.

Finding 5-4: Assertion of foreign copyright by federal agencies in works for which they lack U.S. copyright is inconsistent with the Berne Convention, to which the United States acceded in 1989, as well as prevailing U.S. conflict-of-laws principles.

Recommendation 5-1: Congress should consider amending Section 105(a) of the Copyright Act to allow copyright on software developed by government-owned, government-operated federal laboratories on a prospective basis, subject to a number of limitations, as described in Recommendation 5-2. The amendment should also require that each agency collect appropriate data to determine the impact of such a change.

Recommendation 5-2: Any exclusive software copyright license issued by a government-owned, government-operated federal laboratory should be subject to the following limitations:

- Consideration of the costs and benefits of granting exclusive versus nonexclusive licenses or contributing the relevant work to the public domain, including what is needed to bring the software to practical application or to promote its utilization for the public benefit.
- A limit of 10 years' duration or a shorter period of time sufficient to commercialize the relevant software. A waiver of this time limit could be considered if licensees provided sufficient justification.
- Announcement in the *Federal Register* of the proposed grant of exclusive rights, together with the justification for it, and consideration of public comments made in response to that announcement.

Recommendation 5-3: If Congress does create an exception to Section 105(a) of the Copyright Act for software developed by government-owned, government-operated laboratories, the National Institute of Standards and Technology should commission a study to determine whether and how changing the law has affected the use, dissemination, and commercialization of federally developed software.

Recommendation 5-4: If Congress does not amend Section 105(a) of the Copyright Act to allow government-owned, government-operated laboratories to hold copyright in federally created software, the director of the National Institute of Standards and Technology should develop a uniform federal software contribution agreement that does not depend on copyright, to be made available for use by all federal labs on a voluntary basis.

Recommendation 5-5: Congress should consider repealing the recognition of copyright in standard reference data (SRD) under the SRD Act.

Recommendation 5-6: The Department of Justice's Office of Legal Counsel should issue an advisory opinion to all federal agencies clarifying that in general, foreign copyright is presumed to be unavailable with respect to works covered by the government works exclusion under Section 105(a) of the Copyright Act.

6

Technology Transfer Pathways for Digital Products

Preceding chapters have described policies, regulations, and laws that govern federal laboratories and their role in the development of digital products. The purpose of this chapter is to describe the pathways by which the research, inventions, and data produced by federal labs are commercialized and disseminated to the broader marketplace. The chapter also considers the importance of individual and organizational factors in advancing technology transfer.

Federal labs show considerable heterogeneity in their approaches to technology transfer. The labs have different missions and norms, and the research and technology development efforts across labs, even those within the same federal agency, are seldom coordinated. Moreover, different types of digital products are not always amenable to the same commercialization and dissemination pathways. Thus, the pathway for commercializing or disseminating a particular digital product often depends on both the lab and the type of product.

TECHNOLOGY TRANSFER OFFICES AT THE FEDERAL LABORATORIES

As discussed in Chapter 2, the Stevenson-Wydler Act, 15 U.S.C. § 3710(b), requires each federal laboratory to establish an internal technology transfer office (TTO, also known as an office of research and technology applications [ORTA]) and to support that office with "sufficient" funding. In addition, each lab having 200 or more full-time equivalent (FTE) scientific, engineering, and related technical positions must staff its TTO with at least one FTE position.

In 2017, the National Institute of Standards and Technology (NIST) surveyed federal TTOs to gather data on their budgets, staffing, and resources (Gingrich, 2018). NIST reported that these TTOs receive their funding through a variety of channels: for fiscal year 2016, the funding source for 14 percent of responding TTOs was a specific line item within an agency budget, for 26 percent was overhead, and for 25 percent was a superior office within an agency. Royalty payments alone funded only a small number of responding lab TTOs (2 percent were funded by royalty payments alone), although one-sixth of the responding TTOs reported being funded through a combination of royalty payments and overhead or appropriated funds). TTOs with budgets of more than $5 million had an average of 33.67 FTEs dedicated to technology transfer functions, while those with a budget of less than $1 million had an average of 2.44 FTEs.

The committee also heard from representatives of a number of federal agencies and labs regarding their TTO operations and other technology transfer activities to gain a better understanding of the institutional frameworks and resources for technology transfer within the labs. The committee heard from representatives of four Department of Energy (DOE) labs, one National Science Foundation (NSF) lab, one National Aeronautics and Space Administration (NASA) lab, and one Department of Defense (DOD) lab whose annual TTO budgets ranged from $500,000 to $10 million, with staffing of between 1 and 42 FTEs. Although these labs do not represent the universe of federal labs, they do represent a wide range of internal technology transfer capacity, and they provided both qualitative and quantitative measures of their technology transfer functions and practices.

Three of the labs whose representatives spoke to the committee indicated that more than half of their TTO personnel had science/engineering/medical training, while the staff of two TTOs consisted of individuals with training in business. The staffs of the larger TTOs (19 or more FTEs) included legal personnel, who made up 26 percent of the largest TTO's staff. The staffs of all the TTOs included administrative personnel, generally representing 15 percent or less of the TTO's FTEs but reaching 27 percent in one case. One lab was a federally funded research and development center (FFRDC) administered by a university. This lab maintained its own small TTO (4 FTEs), but also relied on the university's TTO (40 FTEs) for legal and administrative support.

Although the committee spoke only to representatives of a limited number of labs, it does appear that the TTOs' reporting structures vary. In four of the seven labs, the TTO director reports to a senior administrative official at the lab, and in the other three, the TTO director reports to a senior research, science, or technology official. These observations may shed light on the perceived role of the TTO within a lab—whether it is viewed primarily as an administrative office or as part of the research enterprise. It is worth noting that, according to preliminary results of a qualitative study, scientists at federal labs are less likely than their counterparts at universities to "bypass" the TTO (Choi et al., 2020).

Decisions about the dissemination and commercialization of digital products are not always centralized within federal labs. While decisions regarding more explicitly legal forms of technology transfer (e.g., patents, license agreements, cooperative research and development agreements [CRADAs]) are made by a lab's TTO personnel in consultation with its management, decisions about less formal dissemination of technology and knowledge (e.g., data release, scientific publications, open-source software) may be made by the lab's research management, individual research units, or individual investigators. Most studies have focused on formal technology transfer mechanisms, in part because of the greater ease of obtaining data on patenting and CRADAs relative to less formal mechanisms. However, all of these mechanisms are important means of transferring knowledge, know-how, and scientific expertise from the federal labs, and each is discussed in greater detail below.

Finally, although most federal labs operate independently with respect to technology transfer, some agencies have taken steps to coordinate activity among the labs they oversee. In 2007, for example, the national laboratory directors of the 17 DOE labs established the National Laboratory Directors' Council (NLDC) to encourage collaboration and support on issues of common interest to the labs. In May 2015, the NLDC established a new Working Group of National Laboratory Technology Transfer Executives (NLTT) to advise the laboratory directors on issues and opportunities in technology transition, innovation, and commercialization. The NLTT serves as an interface with DOE Headquarters on department-wide issues and opportunities for improving the transition of technologies from the lab into commercial practice.[1] In 2015, DOE established an Office of Technology Transition to coordinate the department's technology transfer activities. The agency also established a Technology Transfer Working Group (TTWG) to improve technology transfer activities, enhance existing processes, and promote consistency of processes across DOE field elements and labs, as required in legislation (42 U.S.C. § 16391). Among other things, the TTWG has developed materials intended to assist labs with technology transfer activities.[2] Despite these initiatives, however, no overarching organization oversees the technology commercialization activities of all of the federal labs or any subset of labs across agency lines.

TECHNOLOGY TRANSFER AND DISSEMINATION PATHWAYS

As with the following chapter on measures of technology transfer and commercialization, it is useful to distinguish among knowledge, invention, and innovation. *Knowledge* is an input into invention and is reflected in, for example, publications or data. *Inventions* are the novel tangible or virtual artifacts of knowledge and can be documented, for example, by patents. Inventions are an input into *innovations*, which are new products, processes, or services introduced to the market (i.e., commercialized). In this section, technology transfer and dissemination pathways for four types of federal laboratory outputs are described: (1) knowledge, (2) data and databases, (3) software, and (4) patentable inventions. An additional pathway—cooperative research arrangements—is also described. Data on the measurement of inputs to innovation (such as publications), inventions, and some of the other technology transfer pathways are described more fully in the next chapter.

---

[1] Email from Richard Rankin, Director, Innovation and Partnerships Office, Lawrence Livermore National Laboratory and then President of the NLTT, dated December 11, 2019.
[2] See https://www.energy.gov/technologytransitions/technology-transfer-working-group-ttwg.

Knowledge

Knowledge from the laboratories, including new discoveries, insights, inventions, and ways of doing things, may serve as inputs into the research and development (R&D) activities of firms that ultimately lead to new digital products introduced to the market. Such knowledge may move both through formal pathways, such as publications, and through such informal channels as conference presentations and professional networks, which several studies have shown to be a potentially important means of transferring knowledge from the lab to the private sector, especially in the software domain (Cohen and Lemley, 2001). Survey data have led some researchers to conclude that publications, conferences, and informal interactions are more important than licenses or cooperative ventures as channels for accessing research from government labs and universities (Cohen et al., 2002).

Researchers at federal labs regularly publish their work in scientific and technical journals. The 2013 Office of Science and Technology Policy (OSTP) memorandum "Promoting Access to Publications Arising from Federally Funded Research" mandates that federal agencies ensure that publications arising from their research activities be made available as broadly as possible on an open-access basis. Since 2008, the National Institutes of Health (NIH) has required that publications arising from all the research it funds, both extramural and intramural, be deposited in its PubMed Central repository within 12 months of publication.[3] As of this writing, PubMed Central contains more than 1 million peer-reviewed articles that are publicly available at no charge. Other agencies, including DOE and DOD, are also implementing measures to make the results of their research publicly available. For example, DOE's Public Access Gateway for Energy and Science (DOE PAGES) is a discovery tool that makes peer-reviewed scientific publications resulting from DOE research publicly accessible within 12 months of publication.[4]

Today, most open-access publication policies are self-executing, requiring little intervention from a lab's TTO or management. In many fields, the scientific publishing industry has largely internalized federal open-access policies, and has adjusted publication agreements to accommodate both the lack of federal copyright in publications by federal employees and the need to make articles publicly available within a designated time period following publication (Contreras, 2013). In fact, in most cases, publishers themselves submit required preprint versions of the articles they will publish to federal open-access databases such as PubMed Central so as to retain control over the release process.

---

[3] See https://publicaccess.nih.gov/policy.htm.
[4] See https://www.osti.gov/pages/.

Data and Databases

Federal laboratories generate vast quantities of observational, experimental, and computational data in fields ranging from meteorology and oceanography, to radio astronomy and particle physics, to epidemiology and population health. Numerous federal policies require the public release and availability of federally created data, and many federal labs have released large quantities of nonclassified data to the public. In its information gathering, the committee heard from no labs that had ever licensed data on a commercial basis.

Some federal data release programs were in place long before current federal open-data policies were enacted. For example, NASA has made its earth science data fully open since 1994, sharing data from satellites and other instruments as soon as they become available. Likewise, since 1992, NIH and its individual institutes have adopted policies requiring the sharing and public release of data arising from genomic and other biomedical research. NIH has led the creation, maintenance, and growth of a genomic data commons that has become a key resource for the global biomedical research community, both public and private (Contreras and Knoppers, 2018).

Federal labs make data publicly available today through multiple online channels. In many cases, labs have created web-based portals through which data can be accessed, searched, downloaded, and used. A large amount of federal data is freely available at data.gov. In some cases, such as NIH's Database of Genotypes and Phenotypes (dbGaP), data are more tightly controlled, and access requests must be approved to ensure that appropriate precautions are taken with respect to individually identifiable information.

That said, large datasets often require substantial maintenance, updating, quality control, annotation, and other associated services. Agencies such as NIH spend upwards of $100 million annually on the curation and hosting of their many datasets (Contreras, 2017; Contreras and Reichman, 2015). Other agencies spend less, and private actors wishing to utilize some publicly accessible government data may need to invest resources to make the data useful in particular commercial contexts.

Input provided to the committee by lab representatives suggests that decisions about the release and curation of federal data are generally not made by a lab's TTO. Rather, those decisions, as well as decisions about the resources committed to putting data in usable form, appear to be made by scientific and technical staff with managerial responsibility for the respective projects. In addition, some larger labs, such as the National Renewable Energy Laboratory (NREL), have developed software applications to facilitate the release of datasets by research groups throughout the lab.[5]

---

[5] See data.nrel.gov.

Software

A wide variety of software is developed at the federal laboratories, from highly specialized scientific programs and instrumentation systems; to data analysis algorithms and data sharing platforms; to programming languages and simulations; to artificial intelligence, statistical models, and machine learning tools; to more consumer-focused desktop and mobile applications. Given this diversity of software types, it is not surprising that the means by which individual lab-developed software programs are disseminated are highly situation dependent.

The principal decision regarding the dissemination of lab-developed software is whether it should be released on an open-source software (OSS) basis or licensed to one or more private-sector firms on a commercial basis.[6] The federal government has adopted an open-source policy that encourages federal agencies to utilize OSS channels for the release of software, and large quantities of lab-developed software have accordingly been distributed under open-source licenses or contribution agreements. Yet concerns have been raised, as discussed in previous chapters, that the financial incentives accompanying exclusive rights may be necessary or desirable to promote the most effective commercialization of some software programs. Labs must thus decide which dissemination route to take with respect to any given software program.[7] (See Box 6-1).

Input provided to the committee by representatives of some of the labs suggests that different labs take different approaches to the decision about whether to release software on an OSS or commercial basis. First, there appears to be no uniform decision maker responsible for this determination. While representatives of several labs stated that new software programs must be reported using a system operated by the lab TTO, the mode of software release can be determined by the individual software developer, the relevant research group or group leader, or a higher-ranking research or administrative official at the lab. Only one lab reported that a representative of the lab's TTO is also involved in making this decision. In most cases, external project funders or sponsors, whether private or governmental, are also consulted regarding the means by which software is to be disseminated, and in some cases, they are largely responsible for this decision.

---

[6] While the lack of federal copyright in software, discussed in Chapter 5, inhibits labs from commercially licensing software that is wholly developed by federal employees, large quantities of software are produced either by employees of government-owned, contractor-operated (GOCO) labs or by federal employees in conjunction with private-sector collaborators, both resulting in software copyrights that can be licensed commercially.

[7] It is important to note that while some software-based inventions may be subject to patent applications and issued patents (see Chapters 4 and 7), most federal lab–developed software is disseminated via software licensing agreements (including OSS licenses).

BOX 6-1
Combining Pathways for Disseminating Software: Goma and CUBIT

One of the missions of Sandia National Laboratories is to design, build, and test components for the nation's nuclear weapons stockpile. To make the development cycles for these components more efficient, the lab has created software tools with which to optimize component designs while minimizing expensive physical prototyping. This kind of "multiphysics" simulation software can be useful in a wide range of manufacturing and industrial processes.

The software developed at Sandia has two main components: the first simulates the complex physics and materials science governing the behavior of an object; the second defines the object in terms of a finely detailed geometric grid or "mesh." This divide in the functionality of the software motivated the lab to commercialize it using separate pathways for each of the two elements.

The physics-simulation component of the software, called Goma, was released on an open-source software (OSS) basis in 2013, and has since been widely adopted by the commercial manufacturing sector, as well as by academia. Sandia considered several factors in making the decision to release Goma under an open-source license, including the existence of laboratory–industry consortia (such as the Nanoparticle Flow Consortium and the Coating Related Manufacturing Processing Consortium) that were eager to contribute to Goma's development. Sandia chose open source as the technology transfer pathway for Goma because of wide interest from nongovernmental entities that could enable a vibrant external development community, as well as the simplicity of software access and external contribution under open-source licensing. The external community engagement would ensure the ongoing robustness of and future improvements to the software.

Crucially, Goma requires a separate software package for creating the geometric meshes used for multiphysics simulation. Both commercial and open-source programs for creating these meshes exist, but are not efficient enough for the advanced work undertaken at Sandia. Sandia therefore developed its own software, called CUBIT, to define these meshes more efficiently. Sandia decided that commercializing CUBIT itself, including user support and broader distribution, would divert too many resources from its mission-centered laboratory work, but one of CUBIT's developers was interested in pursuing his own commercial interest in the software. Sandia therefore licensed the technology behind CUBIT to the researcher's new company (CSimSoft, since acquired by Coreform), and it is now commercially available under the trade name Trelis.

SOURCE: Based on description provided to the committee by Sandia National Laboratories in an email dated March 27, 2020.

Federal lab representatives who addressed the committee described seven different factors their labs consider when deciding how to release software developed at the lab:[8]

- *Programmatic goals*—What are the specific goals of the overall program under which the software was developed?
- *Future development plans*—Does the lab plan to develop and maintain the software in the future? If no further development is planned, it may be important to find a new team—whether an OSS community or commercial partner—to further develop and maintain the software.
- *Purpose of the software*—Is the software broadly applicable or limited to a specialized application? If broad usage by the public is envisioned, OSS release may be most appropriate; if use in specialized equipment produced by a particular vendor is envisioned, a commercial license may be most appropriate.
- *Commercial market/application space*—For software with limited or no commercial market, releasing it as open source can be most beneficial and achieve the widest use since there is no direct cost for acquisition.
- *Third-party dependencies*—Some federal lab–developed software may incorporate third-party code, and any release of that software must comply with contractual and other restrictions on that third-party code. Such restrictions may arise with both OSS code licensed under "copyleft" and similar licenses[9] and proprietary software subject to the terms of a commercial license.
- *Development environment*—Software is developed at federal labs using both such common programming languages as C++, Python, and Java and more specialized development environments. The commercialization pathway for lab-developed software should take into account the overlap between the software's development environment and the language preferences of the target industrial sector.
- *Maturity of the code*—Many software development projects conducted at federal labs are intended to produce only a proof of concept or prototype functionality. These projects are not intended to result in finished products that embody such design principles as security, resilience, and usability. Projects of this nature may require

---

[8] Robert Leland, NREL presentation at open session of committee meeting on December 5, 2019; open session of committee meeting on January 30, 2020 with representatives of DOE's TTWG; and presentations by Mary Monson and Robert Westervelt, Sandia National Laboratories, at open session of committee meeting on March 2, 2020.
[9] For example, the GNU General Public License (GPL) requires that any software program constituting a derivative work of software licensed under the GPL must itself be released under the GPL.

substantial additional investment to be transitioned to usable commercial products. Thus it may be useful to grant exclusive rights in such early-stage code to a private firm that is willing to expend those resources. On the other hand, it may be difficult to find a firm willing to invest the necessary resources to commercialize early-stage code, in which case releasing the code on an OSS basis may be the only practical dissemination mechanism.

Patentable Inventions

Unlike decisions concerning publications, data, and software, those concerning the filing of patent applications and the licensing of patentable inventions at the federal laboratories are handled almost exclusively by lab TTO personnel. All labs have a formalized process through which researchers disclose inventive concepts to the TTO using "invention disclosure" or "technical advance" forms. Officials at the TTO, sometimes in conjunction with legal counsel and science/engineering staff, evaluate these disclosures to determine which inventions merit patent protection. Representatives of the seven labs providing input to the committee reported that 45–90 percent of invention disclosures result in filed patent applications (although they did not differentiate digital products from other inventions).

As noted in Chapter 4, some federal agencies have developed policies regarding the patenting of lab developments. NIH, for example, prepared best practices for patenting and licensing genomic inventions (NIH, 2005).

Once a patent application has been filed, a lab's TTO typically seeks out commercialization partners and licensees for the invention, although the lab's technical personnel are often consulted. Inventions may be licensed on an exclusive or nonexclusive basis. The decision as to which of these licensing routes will be taken depends on a number of factors, including the invention's commercial potential, the number of users that might benefit from it, and the investment required to convert it into a commercial product or application. Some agencies, such as NIH, have expressed preferences for nonexclusive licensing of inventions that have broad applicability or could be utilized as research tools, reserving exclusive licensing for inventions requiring significant investment before they are commercially viable (NIH, 2005). And as discussed in Chapter 4, certain statutory public interest requirements are imposed on government-owned, government-operated (GOGO) federal labs that wish to grant exclusive licenses for lab-owned patents. In Chapter 4, the committee recommends that these requirements be extended to government-owned, contractor-operated (GOCO) labs as well.

Recently, some federal agencies have experimented with new models for identifying potential partners to commercialize federal lab inventions. In 2014–2016, for example, NIH tried using a series of challenges to move early-stage NIH technologies to the market.[10] The winning entries received rights to the technology for a limited period of time.

In some cases, federal labs have determined that the greatest social benefit may arise from making patentable inventions available without charge or formal licensing. In the 1980s, for example, NIH patented the DNA sequence of the HEXA gene associated with Tay-Sachs disease, but chose not to enforce the patent against those who used it in diagnostic tests (Colaianni et al., 2010). More recently, Sandia National Laboratories and the Jet Propulsion Laboratory (JPL) have made certain patents freely available in the fight against COVID-19 pursuant to the Open COVID Pledge.[11]

Cooperative Research Arrangements

An additional important pathway for commercialization of federally developed digital products is the use of cooperative research arrangements, which include formal CRADAs, joint ventures, and other research or development arrangements between federal laboratories and both universities and industry partners. Indeed, researchers have suggested that cooperative research arrangements such as CRADAs are "the single most important channel" for private firms to acquire the underlying inventions[12] that lead to commercialized innovations (Arora et al., 2016). As discussed in more detail in Chapter 7, in 2016 there were more than 11,600 active CRADAs across the federal lab system (NIST, 2019a). Under these arrangements, lab partners provide personnel, research funds, or in-kind contributions, while the lab provides facilities, equipment, or intellectual property. Information generated under CRADAs may be protected from public disclosure for up to 5 years, and the intellectual property that results from the joint research generally belongs to the private firm.

Researchers have shown that lab technologies are often far from commercialization, and thus require a considerable amount of codevelopment through cooperative research arrangements before being ready for the market (Ham and Mowery, 1995; Choudhry and Ponzio, 2020). There is also evidence that, relative to other mechanisms, CRADAs lead to higher levels of patenting for both the federal labs and their industrial lab partners, most likely because of the more intensive collaboration that occurs under CRADAs (Adams et al., 2003).[13]

---

[10] These challenges include the Breast Cancer Startup Challenge, Nanotechnology Startup in Cancer, and Neurostartup run by the Center for Advancing Innovation in partnership with the National Cancer Institute at NIH. See, e.g., Neurostartupchallenge.org.

[11] See opencovidplege.org.

[12] Inventions are to be distinguished from the knowledge inputs into invention, for which, as noted above, the most pervasive pathways from public research institutions to industry are reported to be publications, public meetings, informal information exchange, and consulting (Cohen et al., 2002).

[13] Similar to CRADAs, NASA's agreements, called Space Act Agreements (SAAs), were authorized by Congress under the National Aeronautics and Space Act (51 U.S.C. § 20113[e]).

TECHNOLOGY TRANSFER/COMMERCIALIZATION ECOSYSTEM ENABLERS

R&D activities are part of a broader innovation ecosystem. Federal agencies have implemented numerous programs to promote entrepreneurship at the federal laboratories, to enhance public awareness of available lab expertise and technology, to transition technologies from lab to market, to build partnerships with local communities, and to promote economic growth.

For example, Sandia and Oak Ridge National Laboratory have established science and technology parks, and many DOD labs have partner intermediaries, such as Techlink, located at Montana State University, which serves as a partnership intermediary for technology transfer. DOE has established an internal I-Corps program that provides entrepreneurial services and training to researchers within the department's federal labs. This program pairs researchers with industry mentors to foster a culture of market awareness within the lab and encourage lab employees to undertake entrepreneurial activities. DOE also recently initiated a Technology Commercialization Fund to leverage R&D funding in the applied energy programs to assist in the commercialization of promising energy technologies developed at DOE labs.

In addition, a number of agencies, including DOE, NIH, and DOD, offer postdoctoral fellowships to train, encourage, network, and mentor innovators through such programs as Cyclotron Road at Lawrence Berkeley National Laboratory.[14] And the Department of Health and Human Services (HHS) has established an Entrepreneurs-in-Residence program to help identify, evaluate, and support the development of startups utilizing technology developed or funded by the agency.[15]

The intent and spirit of these programs are to be applauded, although the committee heard little empirical evidence regarding their success in enhancing technology transfer from the labs. Moreover, most of these programs were introduced relatively recently, so it is difficult to determine their success at this time.

INCENTIVES FOR SCIENTISTS AND ENGINEERS TO ENGAGE IN TECHNOLOGY TRANSFER AT FEDERAL LABORATORIES

The literature on university technology transfer identifies several individual and organizational factors that are also likely to influence technology transfer at federal laboratories: (1) individual financial and nonfinancial incentives; (2) social networks; (3) organizational structure, culture, and support for technology transfer; (4) relations between scientists and the TTO/administration and other aspects of organizational justice; (5) identity as a

---

[14] Ilan Gur, Activate, Presentation to the Committee, December 6, 2019.
[15] See https://www.hhs.gov/cto/initiatives/entrepreneurs-in-residence/index.html.

researcher or entrepreneur; (6) role conflict; (7) work–life balance; and (8) championing and leadership. The main focus below is on the first of these factors.

Financial incentives for researchers are reflected in a lab's "royalty distribution formula," which stipulates the fraction of revenue from a licensing transaction that is allocated to the researcher(s) who developed the licensed technology. Studies of university researchers suggest that universities allocating a higher percentage of royalty payments to faculty members garner greater licensing revenues (Lach and Schankerman, 2004; Link and Siegel, 2005). Another study found that attractive financial incentives for faculty help a university attract more productive, commercially oriented researchers (Jensen et al., 2003). And financial incentives and bonuses for TTO employees have been found to increase TTO licensing revenue (Belenzon and Schankerman, 2009).

In considering the role of financial incentives in the context of federal labs, it is of course important to be mindful of several institutional differences between the labs and universities. One example is wage differentials between university and federal lab scientists. Another important difference is that university scientists may be required to secure grants to support some or all of their salary, a requirement generally not faced by their federal lab counterparts. Still another is that federal rules regarding conflicts of interest may constrain both lab researchers and labs themselves from participating in the financial gains of their licensees and from forming startup companies based on licensed technology, as do many university researchers and universities. Finally, federal lab scientists have important roles and priorities other than commercialization, including work furthering the primary governmental missions of the individual labs and agencies, much of which holds no potential for commercialization.

In addition, intellectual property rights that facilitate commercialization can challenge scientific disclosure norms. As identified in the university context, university researchers traditionally have published and presented their scientific findings as soon as possible, in accordance with communal norms promoting the prompt and open sharing of data. Since passage of the Bayh-Dole Act, compliance with patent novelty rules generally has necessitated that university TTOs and restrictive terms in industry sponsorship agreements encourage or require researchers to delay publishing and presenting their work until a patent application has been filed, and sometimes even longer than that (Bagley, 2006). Thus, the unforgiving nature of the patent novelty rules may hamper early public disclosure and even dictate the pace, form, and scope of discourse and disclosure. These factors may explain in part recent findings that federal lab scientists are not highly incentivized to engage in technology transfer and may even experience cognitive dissonance in pursuing entrepreneurial activities (Choi et al., 2020).

Nonfinancial rewards may also be important to researchers. Some universities have started to adapt promotion and tenure and remuneration systems for academics so that commercialization activities are valued.[16] The desire to have social impact, peer recognition, and career advancement may be an important motivator for researchers as well (Cohen et al., 2020). Indeed, the committee heard evidence that such nonfinanical rewards may be important to researchers at federal labs, and that it is important for efforts to increase technology transfer and commercialization to take into account the relevant support needs, such as allowing conference attendance and participation.

Research on "star" university life science researchers and biotech startups shows that social networks may also play a role in technology transfer (Zucker and Darby, 2001; Powell and Owen-Smith, 1998). A recent study found that championing by department chairs/principal investigators (PIs)/center directors is a powerful enabler of technology transfer at both federal labs and universities (Choi et al., 2020).

Sandia was one of the first labs to establish a sabbatical program for lab employees, officially called the Entrepreneurial Separation to Transfer Technology program, to enable them to pursue business ideas in the community. In operation for more than 25 years, this program allows staff to leave the lab with a guaranteed job if they return within 2 years. Since 1994, the program has helped 162 employees—74 who started new companies and 88 who expanded companies—bring business ideas into their communities, primarily in New Mexico. Other federal labs offer similar sabbatical opportunities.

One important but understudied issue relating to the dissemination of federal lab technology is the role played by postdoctoral fellows and other junior members of the research team. Programs to support technology transfer as a career path for postdocs, such as the Technology Transfer Ambassadors Program at the National Cancer Institute, may help transfer technology out of the lab.[17] However, a recent study found that postdocs at federal labs would like to engage in technology transfer but are not encouraged to do so by some PIs (Choi et al., 2020).

FINDINGS AND RECOMMENDATIONS

Finding 6-1: Although the approaches taken by federal laboratories to the dissemination and commercialization of digital publications and data are generally consistent, the approaches taken with respect to software vary across labs.

Finding 6-2: Studies of individual and organizational factors in university technology transfer have yielded insights on the importance

---

[16] Based on a survey of North American institutions, Stevens and colleagues (2011) report that 16 major universities in the United States and Canada considered patents and commercialization in tenure and promotion decisions.
[17] https://techtransfer.cancer.gov/aboutttc/ambassadors#:~:text=The%20NCI%20Technology%20Transfer%20Ambassadors,development%2C%20commercialization%2C%20and%20entrepreneurship.

of incentives (both financial and nonfinancial), championing, and other managerial practices in stimulating technology commercialization and entrepreneurship, but there have been few such studies of managerial practices in the federal laboratory context.

Recommendation 6-1: The Federal Interagency Working Group on Technology Transfer should develop a set of written best practices for federal laboratories to use in determining dissemination pathways for lab-developed software.

Recommendation 6-2: An appropriate federal agency should conduct a study of the potential impact of different incentive and organizational factors on the motivation of federal laboratory researchers to engage in technology transfer and commercialization and the success of such efforts. Federal labs should use the results of this study when considering changes to their incentive structure and organizational practices.

7

Measuring the Commercialization of Digital Products from Federal Laboratories

Assessing the commercialization of federal laboratories' digital products requires a broad range of data, including measures of inputs into lab inventions (e.g., basic research and knowledge creation, research and development [R&D] effort, and data); data on lab discoveries and inventions; and metrics on the subsequent economic and social impacts of new products, processes, and services.

Currently available data permit only a limited understanding of the commercialization of digital products from federal labs. Data on commercialized products, processes, and services produced from knowledge or inventions created in federal labs—including digital products—are extremely limited, and no existing metrics capture the longer-term economic impact of these outputs. Researchers are generally limited to measuring inputs into invention (e.g., R&D spending, knowledge transfer via publications), some evidence of inventions (invention disclosures, patent applications filed, patents issued), and limited metrics for two pathways by which knowledge and technology are transferred out of the labs (licenses and cooperative agreements). Moreover, data on different dimensions of technology transfer (e.g., patents or licenses) are reported only at the agency level, not at the lab level. There also are inherent difficulties in measuring innovation stemming from digital products, which is likely to be intangible. For example, there are only limited quantitative measures for the large amounts of software and data released by federal labs and the individual research groups and scientists within them. Creating additional challenges is that digital products, particularly software, are often bundled with nondigital products.

This chapter reviews the best available measures for these data, and presents the committee's proposal for additional methods and measures for assessing the commercialization of digital products from federal labs.

OVERVIEW AND ASSESSMENT OF AVAILABLE DATA

Federal agencies generally rely on such metrics as licensing income and numbers of patent applications and issued patents to measure the benefit of their technology transfer programs, despite the known limitations of these metrics (Choudhry and Ponzio, 2020). Over the past two decades, the principal federal report on technology transfer at the federal laboratories has been compiled annually by the National Institute of Standards and Technology (NIST). Over time, the breadth of data included in this report has expanded, but the report still does not capture the range of data needed.

Under the Technology Transfer Commercialization Act of 2000 (Pub. L. No. 106-404), federal agencies are required to report technology transfer activities at their labs, and the secretary of commerce includes this information in an annual report on technology transfer to Congress (Pub. L. No. 106-404). Specifically, agencies are required under this statute to report annually information on patents, licenses, royalty income, cooperative research agreements, and anything else relevant to their technology transfer efforts (Pub. L. No. 106-404, §§ 3710[f]–[g]).[1]

A 2011 presidential memorandum titled "Accelerating Technology Transfer and Commercialization of Federal Research in Support of High-Growth Businesses" directed the secretary of commerce to work with other entities, including the Interagency Working Group on Technology Transfer (IAWGTT) and the National Science Foundation's (NSF's) National Center for Science and Engineering Statistics (NCSES), to "improve and expand" metrics in the annual federal technology transfer summary report (Executive Office of the President, 2011). In response, the IAWGTT developed a number of new, mandatory metrics, including number of startups created; number of patents granted, by technology area and agency; science and engineering (S&E) publications, by technology area and agency; citations of S&E articles in U.S. patents, by technology area, article author sector, and agency; and number of technology transfer impact studies completed. In addition, the IAWGTT recommended that federal agencies include measures of the number of software programs created and downloaded (IAWGTT, 2012). The range of data included in the annual technology transfer report has expanded and now includes some of the IAWGTT's required measures. The latest report, covering fiscal year (FY) 2016 and published in September 2019, includes the number of patents issued, by selected technology area; the number of invention disclosures, by agency; the number of published S&E articles authored or coauthored by federal lab employees; and the number of these articles cited in patents, which provides a measure of the commercial relevance of a publication (NIST, 2019a).

---

[1] Academic studies also provide occasional insight into technology transfer at federal labs. See, e.g., Adams et al., 2002; Feldman and Lemley, 2018.

Sample of Data in the Fiscal Year 2016 Technology Transfer Report for Federal Laboratories

This section provides a look at some of the key statistics in the FY 2016 technology transfer report to set the stage for an assessment of the strengths and weaknesses of the data currently provided.

Table 7-1 presents some of the key statistics in the NIST technology transfer report for the four agencies with the largest federal laboratory budgets. These statistics are not confined to digital products, and they represent a mix of government-owned, government-operated (GOGO) and government-owned, contractor-operated (GOCO) labs. (Most Department of Health and Human Services [HHS] and Department of Defense [DOD] labs are GOGOs, most Department of Energy [DOE] labs are GOCOs, and the National Aeronautics and Space Administration [NASA] labs are evenly split between GOGOs and GOCOs.) These statistics include a breakdown of new invention disclosures, patent applications filed, and patents issued, by technology area and both by individual agency and in the aggregate. The technology transfer report notes the percentage of patents issued to federal agencies, by technology area, based on a fractional count of patents.[2] In FY 2016, about 10 percent of federal patents were in the field of measurement, while nearly one-fourth were in biomedical fields.

Data in the report also show that cooperative research and development agreements (CRADAs) and other collaborative arrangements for engagement between the labs and outside organizations were increasing, while in FY 2016, most other technology transfer mechanisms remained at the same level, increasing or decreasing only slightly, with the total number of active CRADAs for all agencies numbering more than 11,600 (NIST, 2019a). HHS labs accounted for the bulk of federal lab licensing income—73 percent of the total—and HHS, DOE, and DOD collectively accounted for nearly all of the royalty income from licenses for the federal government (NIST, 2019a). It should be noted that, although CRADAs are obviously an important mechanism for technology transfer, the statistics on invention disclosures, patents, and licenses do not reflect data for the patenting and licensing activities of the CRADAs themselves, reflecting a significant gap in reporting.

Although these data are useful, in many ways they raise more questions than they answer, as discussed below.

Assessment of Current Metrics on Technology Transfer

Although federal laboratories are typically engaged in the creation of knowledge and the generation of inventions, much of that work is not reflected in the annual technology transfer report, which focuses on patents, licenses, and

---

[2] NIST credits patents on a fractional-count basis, so that each federal agency receives a fraction of the credit when there are assignees from multiple agencies.

TABLE 7-1 Federal Laboratory Technology Transfer Metrics in the National Institute of Standards and Technology's Annual Report for the Four Largest Agencies (in terms of federal lab budgets), Fiscal Year 2016

Agency	GOGO and GOCO R&D Budget (millions of dollars)	GOCO Share of GOGO/GOCO R&D Budget (percent)	Number of New Invention Disclosures	Number of Patent Applications Filed	Number of Patents Issued	Number of Active Licenses	Total License Income (thousands of dollars)	Number of Active CRADAs
DOD	18,567	9	874	941	665	515	6,205	3,125
DOE	8,152	88	1,760	999	856	5,410	31,149	739
HHS	7,642	7	320	269	579	1,750	132,833	590
NASA	3,314	46	1,554	129	103	452	3,149	12

NOTE: CRADA = cooperative research and development agreement; DOD = Department of Defense; DOE = Department of Energy; GOCO = government-owned, contractor-operated; GOGO = government-owned, government-operated; HHS = Department of Health and Human Services; NASA = National Aeronautics and Space Administration; R&D = research and development.
SOURCE: National Institute of Standards and Technology (NIST, 2019a).

CRADAs. These metrics are heavily weighted toward formal activities and in most cases reflect only those cases in which a transfer of money occurs. No data are collected on software or data compilations that are made freely available through open-source portals. The only information collected on intellectual property created by labs relates to patents, and no information is collected on copyright, even for GOCO labs that are able to claim copyright in software and other works of authorship. Nor are any systematic data collected on innovations (i.e., commercialized products, processes, and services) that build less formally on the knowledge and inventions that flow from federal labs. And there are no data on the number of startups created or their economic impact.[3] Of course, the aggregate data reported also do not allow one to identify technology transfer or even publications and citations relating specifically to digital products at the agency or federal lab level.

The measures currently available, although collected from the labs, are reported only at the agency level. Disaggregated data would help policy makers understand how different policies and practices across the federal labs affect the ability and propensity of each lab to ensure that knowledge and inventions are made available. Although inherent differences across agencies make cross-lab comparisons difficult, disaggregated data could also provide information about individual labs over time. In some instances, however, disaggregating data may still leave gaps in understanding. This is the case, for example, with patents given the changing patent landscape and the limited extent to which software is even patented.

Patent Activity

The annual technology transfer report collects information about invention disclosures and patents, but patents may not be a reliable measure of innovation in digital products, specifically software. As described in Chapter 4 and noted above, many software inventions are not patented. Given the complexities of patent claim drafting, it is also difficult to identify software patents that do exist (Rai et al., 2009). In addition, the technological and economic importance of patents varies substantially, and indeed, most patents are never commercialized (Sichelman, 2010).

The committee analyzed the patents for the laboratories of three agencies—DOE, DOD, and NASA—for the period 1980–2014[4] using the patent classes identified as software by previous researchers (Graham and Vishnubhakat, 2013). The committee's analysis illustrates a number of points that highlight the

---

[3] The FY 2016 technology transfer report also indicates that while most agencies have a long history of working with startups, few agencies have established "systematic methods to identify and track the startup companies they nurture" (NIST, 2019a).

[4] The committee also examined software patents for HHS, which includes the National Institutes of Health (NIH), Centers for Disease Control and Prevention (CDC), and Food and Drug Administration (FDA). Although the labs of these agencies have a large number of patents, attributable mostly to NIH, they have too few software patents to merit reporting here.

importance of disaggregating data. First, software patenting, especially by DOE and DOD, is significant. In total, these three agencies were issued almost 400 software patents in 2014, compared with close to 700 software patents for all American universities. Second, as shown in Figures 7-1 and 7-2, there are enormous differences in patenting behavior across labs within an agency, even after normalizing for the number of employees. Third, the committee's analysis revealed that software patent activity has varied considerably over time, being most intensive between the mid-1990s and early 2000s for DOE and DOD labs, corresponding roughly to the final 10 years or so of what is referred to as the "patent surge" in the United States (see Figures 7-3 and 7-4). Disaggregating data also makes it possible to explore variations among different types of labs. DOE labs, for instance, are a mix of fundamental research labs, labs that primarily operate user facilities, applied engineering labs, and nuclear weapons labs.

Comparing forward citations to software patents across the three agencies' labs since 2000, the average, normalized numbers of citations to patents

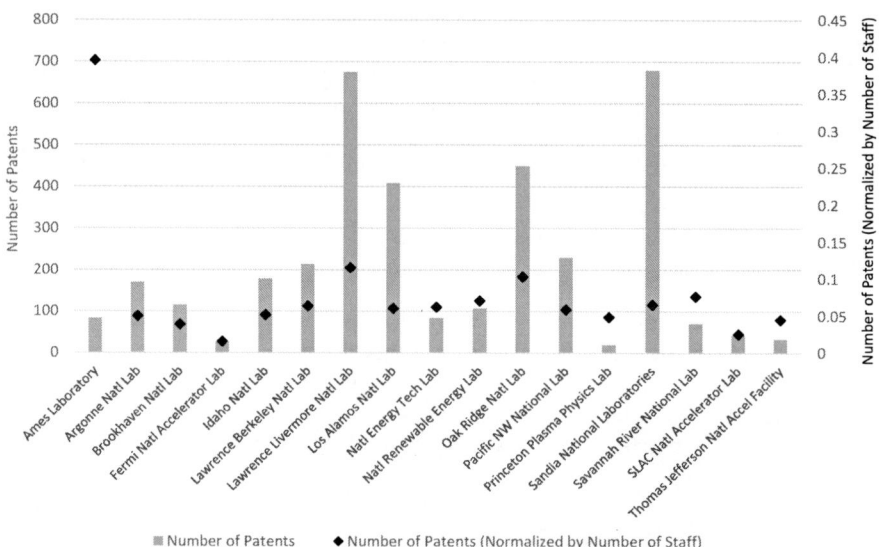

FIGURE 7-1 Software patents by Department of Energy laboratories, normalized by number of employees, 2014.
NOTE: DOE patents were identified by searching Google Patents for the Department of Energy, the names of labs, and the names of contractor operators of labs. When the lab was not identified, it was assigned based on the inventor's location.
SOURCE: Committee calculations based on data from the Office of Scientific and Technical Information (OSTI) (https://www.osti.gov/) and the European Patent Office's World Patent Statistical Database (PatStat) (https://data.epo.org/expert-services/index.html).

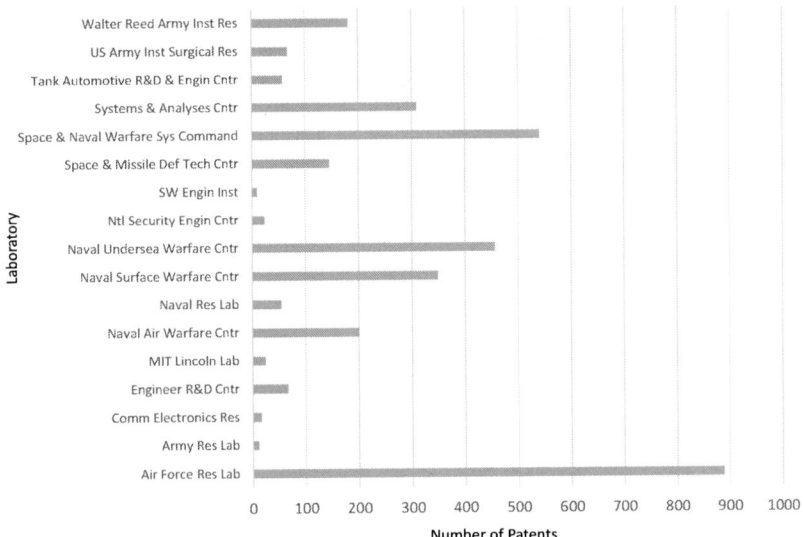

FIGURE 7-2 Software patents by Department of Defense laboratories (employee counts not available), 2014.
NOTE: DOD patents were identified by searching for Department of Defense, Air Force, Army, and Navy in the assignee fields in the Google Patents search panel and matched to individual labs based on the inventor's location. Only about half of the 6,400 DOD patents could be matched to a lab.
SOURCE: Committee calculations based on data from Google Patents (https://patents.google.com/).

for the labs of, respectively, DOE, DOD, and NASA are 1.55, 0.95, and 1.36. Forward citations are the number of patents in the future that cite the invention, and are considered a good measure of a patent's usefulness or value (Trajtenberg, 1990). Although it is not possible to claim that the patents of DOE labs are more commercially valuable or significant than, say, those of DOD labs, such a substantial difference raises questions about the private-sector value or commercial viability of software patents or the effectiveness of technology transfer operations of one agency compared with another.

Licenses

The NIST report devotes a great deal of attention to licenses. Unfortunately, these aggregate, agency-level data are not disaggregated according to the character of the underlying invention, making it impossible to determine how many of these licenses relate to digital products, nor are the data reported for individual laboratories. As noted earlier, the data in Table 7-1 show that HHS labs

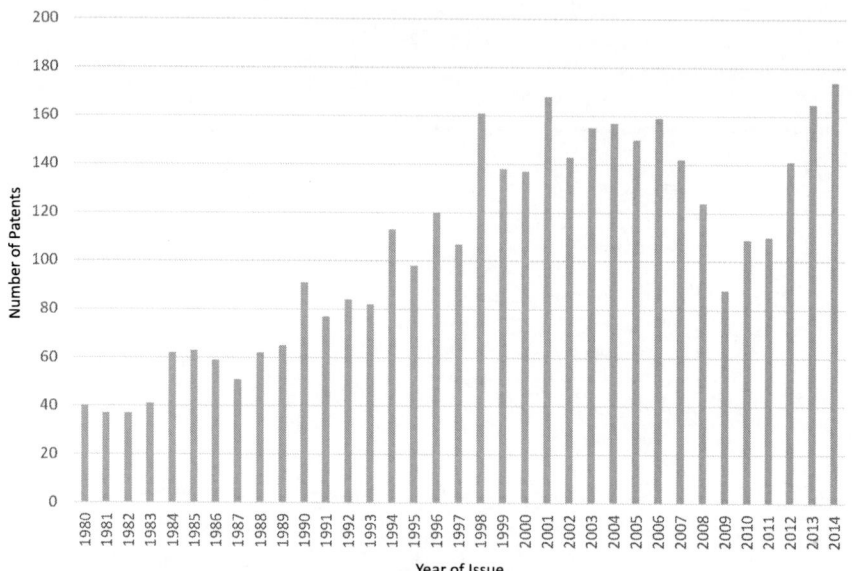

FIGURE 7-3 Software patents by Department of Energy laboratories, by year (1980–2014).
SOURCE: Committee calculations based on data from the Office of Scientific and Technical Information (OSTI) (https://www.osti.gov/) and the European Patent Office's World Patent Statistical Database (PatStat) (https://data.epo.org/expert-services/index.html).

accounted for the bulk (73 percent) of federal lab licensing income in FY 2016, which raises questions about how this total is distributed among the HHS labs, the mix of technologies being licensed, and whether there are differences between GOGOs and GOCOs.

In April 2020, NIST's Technology Partnership Office, working with the IAWGTT, released a list of "optional" metrics for agencies to report. Particularly relevant to digital products, the list includes software licenses executed, software products available for licensing, and copyright licenses executed. Because these additional metrics are optional, however, they are less likely to be implemented widely relative to the required metrics, and their impact on understanding of the commercialization of digital products is therefore uncertain at best.

Participation in Cooperative Research and Development Agreements

Data on CRADAs are currently included in the NIST report on an agency-wide basis. Cooperative arrangements generally, and CRADAs in

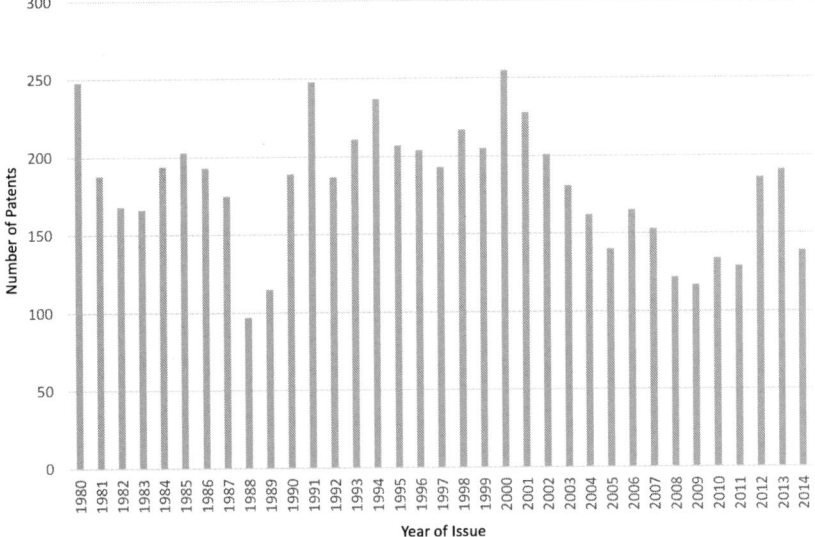

FIGURE 7-4 Software patents by Department of Defense laboratories, by year (1980–2014).
SOURCE: Committee calculations based on data from Google Patents (https://patents.google.com/).

particular, are widely recognized as important mechanisms for technology transfer from the federal laboratories to industry and other organizations (Adams et al., 2003; Arora et al., 2016). CRADAs are associated with higher levels of company patenting compared with other technology transfer mechanisms, most likely as a result of the more intensive collaboration between labs and companies under these agreements (Adams et al., 2003). Because information on CRADAs is not disaggregated by type of technology, however, it is impossible to know their importance for digital technologies. And again, the failure to disaggregate the data by lab is an important shortcoming.

In addition, a more comprehensive accounting of innovation and commercialization outcomes arising from CRADAs and other cooperative arrangements between federal labs and the private sector is needed to assess the effectiveness of these arrangements. This accounting needs to encompass the full range of outcomes, including both failures and successes, so the determinants of performance can be assessed. Also important are data on cooperative ventures by startups and on woman- and minority-owned businesses to ensure that access to the labs' resources has been equitable and fair.

Publications, Conferences, and Informal Information Exchange

As described in Chapter 6, the contributions of federal laboratories to private-sector innovations extend beyond patents, licenses, and cooperative research arrangements. Previous studies of industrial innovation have shown that knowledge transfer via published papers and reports, public conferences and meetings, informal information exchange, and consulting is the key means by which government and university research affects industrial innovation (Cohen et al., 2002). Although NIST's annual technology transfer report does include S&E publications, these data are reported at the government-wide level, thus not allowing analysis by lab, let alone any insight into the substance of the publications and whether they relate to digital products. NIST acknowledges that "a uniform tracking system for S&E articles across all federal agencies does not exist" (NIST, 2019a, p. 14), nor does there exist a tracking system for more informal knowledge transfers. Understanding the role of the federal labs' contributions to the nation's knowledge capital, particularly via publications, is especially important in light of the secular decline of public firms' participation in publishable science over the past 30 years in the United States (Arora et al., 2016).

The production of publications has increased substantially at many labs. DOE labs in particular have seen a significant increase in the last 25 years, perhaps resulting from an infusion of resources or shifts in scientific domains within these labs (Sugimoto, 2020). Several federal agencies have created portals to make publications from their lab researchers and grantees more accessible, likely increasing the importance of this pathway for technology transfer from the labs, and hence the need to better understand the impact of publications. Venues for these publications include the National Library of Medicine's PubMed Central[5] and DOE's Public Access Gateway for Energy and Science (DOE PAGES).[6] More than 65,000 publicly available full-text journal articles and manuscripts are available through DOE PAGES, and this number is expected to grow by about 20,000–30,000 articles and manuscripts per year. DOE PAGES also offers a reference/citation tool that enables users to track the impact of an article through citations in other publications, including articles in conference proceedings and journal articles as well as patents.

Datasets and Software Code

Other important contributors to private-sector innovation include datasets and software code. Although datasets may provide the basis for laboratory inventions, they are also transferred out of the labs through data downloads, which are not reported. In addition, software code produced in a lab may contribute to further inventions in the lab or may be downloaded for use

---

[5] Access at https://support.nlm.nih.gov/knowledgebase/article/KA-03247/en-us.
[6] Access at https://www.osti.gov/pages/.

outside the lab, and as with datasets, these downloads are not reported or made publicly available. Better understanding of the existence, use, and impact of datasets and software code is critical to understanding the commercialization of the digital products of the labs.

Although statistics on knowledge transfers, data downloads, and software downloads are not reported in the annual technology transfer reports, the committee was able to compile some limited information on publications, datasets, and software based on data from Web of Science, data.gov, and code.gov. These data are presented in Table 7-2, which shows that a very large volume of transfer from labs occurs through such products as these rather than through traditional patenting and licensing channels. As with other fragmentary available data, these are more suggestive than conclusive, since they are not disaggregated by lab.

The dissemination of data collected through experiments and other functions of the federal labs is another critical component of knowledge sharing within the innovation process; however, information on data downloads is not included in the technology transfer report.[7] Despite that omission, some agencies collect information on data use, which would be useful if systematically reported. For example, NASA gathers earth observation data and makes these data usable by the public, academia, and industry. NASA tracks daily visits to its open data portal and its application programming interface (API) portal, which help application developers use these data; API.nasa.gov had 9 million hits in May 2019 alone. In addition to its open data portal, NASA operates an Earth Observing System Data Information System (EOSDIS) and Planetary Data System. In 2018, EOSDIS held approximately 37 petabytes of data and delivered more than 1.6 billion data products to more than 4.1 million users around the world. NASA

TABLE 7-2 Innovation Inputs from Federal Researchers and Laboratories

Agency	Inputs to Innovation			
	Datasets	Software Code	Cumulative Publications	Publications, 2019
DOD	378	17	246,703	6,194
DOE	2,868	1,948	552,452	19,052
HHS	2,041	179	427,339*	13,289*
NASA	32,089	1,257	167,315	5,558

NOTES: Data are reported for the agencies whose labs have the largest research and development budgets. DOD = Department of Defense; DOE = Department of Energy; HHS = Department of Health and Human Services; NASA = National Aeronautics and Space Administration. * Indicates data for the National Institutes of Health alone.
SOURCE: Datasets at data.gov; source code from code.gov; publication data from Web of Science with author or co-author affiliation from the federal agency.

---

[7] Included in the list of "optional" metrics for agencies that was released in April 2020 by NIST's Technology Partnership Office, working with the IAWGTT, was the number of datasets open to the public.

collects metrics across all the EOSDIS distributed active data centers and publishes an annual report of EOSDIS metrics.[8] There is evidence of commercial products stemming from NASA's data and software, such as from WebWorldWind, which has been used "to monitor weather patterns, visualize cities and terrain, track vehicle movement, analyze geospatial data, and educate humanity about Earth."[9]

Other agencies not included among the four in Table 7-2 also provide a substantial number of datasets, most of which are available for public use. For example, the Department of the Interior has more than 80,000 datasets, and NIST, the National Oceanic and Atmospheric Administration, and the National Telecommunications and Information Administration's Institute for Telecommunication Sciences possess nearly 40,000 datasets.

Although measuring the number of datasets is helpful, it is more important to understand the degree to which they are being utilized outside of the government. Without an idea of the number of downloads or dataset citations or, better yet, some sense of how they are contributing to innovation, understanding the economic value of the data produced by federal labs with any accuracy is impossible.[10] An additional complicating factor is that once downloaded, these data may be made available on cloud platforms, where there could be widespread additional dissemination without downloading.

Assessing the impact of federally created software on innovation and commercialization can be challenging because the software itself is not typically deployed commercially, but instead enables the development of commercial products, processes, or services. For example, DOE acknowledged challenges in tracking the impact of model simulations on future innovations and products downstream (Lally, 2019). The development of additional APIs and expansion of platforms such as GitHub over the past few years have made it easier to assess the value of federally created software, including the extent of its use and reuse, as well as the interconnections among open-source networks (Keller et al., 2018). NASA has 267 repositories posted on Github.nasa.gov and collects data using scripts on which projects have the most interaction.

Although a number of government agencies and federal labs have implemented policies with respect to collecting and analyzing how their knowledge and information, including digital products, are being used by the private sector, this information is not universally collected. Exemplar agencies, such as DOE, are employing common platforms such as DOE.code[11] and code.gov to consolidate information on the number of downloads from their software code depositories. Similarly, NASA has implemented an internally

---

[8] See https://earthdata.nasa.gov/eosdis/system-performance.
[9] See https://worldwind.arc.nasa.gov/web/.
[10] It is also difficult to predict potential uses for the data in the future. For example, although Landsat maps were originally designed for agricultural applications, they provided valuable information that aided in gold discovery, such that the rate of significant gold discoveries doubled after a region had been mapped (Nagaraj, 2018).
[11] Access at https://www.osti.gov/doecode/.

facing software release program to streamline and standardize the review process for software across all 10 field centers and improve its ability to track downloads of NASA's public data, software, and APIs (Murphy, 2019). NASA is an exemplar in making its software available and may serve as a model for other agencies to follow in making their software more easily discovered.

Impacts beyond Technology Transfer

As noted in the case of datasets and software, any understanding of the contributions of the federal laboratories to innovation requires understanding how their outputs are utilized outside the lab. No metrics are collected that measure the effect of technology transfer on the recipient organization or the broader economic or societal impact of research at federal labs (Link et al., 2019).

Several federal agencies have conducted their own studies to determine the economic impact of their labs. While not generalizable, these individual economic impact reports can inform data collection and analysis methodologies, contribute to the improvement of technology transfer and commercialization programs, provide a better understanding of the economic and other impacts of specific technologies, and improve technology transfer and commercialization programs (Conover et al., 2010; O'Connor et al., 2019).

These reports may be particularly helpful in assessing the value of data, which are more challenging to value than conventional assets as there is no uniformly established framework for capturing their value (Coyle et al., 2020). For example, a study of the U.S. Geological Survey's LANDSAT images estimates that LANDSAT provided users an annual benefit of $2.19 billion in 2011, $1.79 billion of which redounded to U.S. users (Miller et al., 2013). An update in 2019 estimates the benefit to be $3.45 billion in 2017, with U.S. users accounting for $2.06 billion of that total (Straub et al., 2019). A 2019 report on the U.S. Air Force's Global Positioning System (GPS) shows such benefits as "productivity gains from new and existing products and services, improvements in quality, increases in personal enjoyment, and environmental and public health impacts" (O'Connor et al., 2019, p. ES-2). And a 2013 study released by the Battelle Institute estimates that the federal investment in Human Genome Project–related genomics research has resulted in a total U.S. economic impact of nearly $1 trillion since 1988 (Battelle Technology Partnership Practice, 2013).

PROPOSED NEW METRICS

As discussed above, metrics presented in NIST's annual technology transfer report do not provide sufficient information to conduct a comprehensive assessment of the effectiveness of federal laboratory technology transfer activities with respect to digital products and their subsequent commercialization. Moreover, separate metrics are not currently collected for digital products. The development of metrics for such a specific category will be challenging given the wide array of digital products arising from research at the federal labs and the combination of components that may exist within a single digital product.

New approaches and measures would enable a more comprehensive evaluation of the effectiveness of the federal labs' technology transfer and commercialization activities, both as they relate to digital products and more broadly. As a first consideration, it is important to note that most of the data discussed above—R&D spending, patents, publications, CRADAs—do not reflect the development of new products, processes, or services (i.e., innovations). Rather, they reflect either measures of inputs into inventions or innovations (e.g., publications) or inventions themselves (e.g., patents, software). These measures do not reveal what or how many new products, processes, or services were actually developed and commercialized on the basis of these inputs. To obtain such information, it is necessary to survey firms whose commercialization efforts build on the knowledge and inventions derived from the labs (Link et al., 2019). Such a survey of firms need not be a stand-alone survey, but could be added to NSF's current corporate R&D surveys.[12]

Survey questions concerning digital products might cover two broad areas: (1) the knowledge flows from federal labs that contribute to firms' R&D and related efforts, and (2) the acquisition and commercialization of developed inventions (patented and not) from the federal labs.

Survey Questions Concerning Knowledge Flows

Survey questions concerning flows of knowledge from federal laboratories into a firm's R&D operations might best be targeted to companies' R&D unit managers or directors (Cohen et al., 2002). Questions could include, for example, whether any of a number of possible sources provided information, data, or knowledge that either (1) suggested a new R&D project, (2) contributed to the completion of an existing project, or (3) resulted in process improvements. In addition to federal labs, other possible sources might include other firms (e.g., buyers, suppliers, competitors), contractors, or universities. Inquiring about such other sources would enable assessment of the importance of knowledge originating from the federal labs and comparison of the importance of the labs and other sources as providers of such knowledge. A question could also be asked regarding the amount of time and effort that was required to "clean up" lab-developed datasets to make them usable for further development and commercialization.

Additional questions regarding the contributions of the federal labs to companies' R&D could include the percentage of a firm's R&D projects that make use of various types of outputs, including research findings, techniques, instruments, software, and data, from the labs (or other sources), and the frequency with which federal lab outputs contribute to companies' R&D projects

---

[12] The Annual Business Survey, undertaken by NCSES, is an example of an existing survey concerned with corporate R&D and innovation. See https://www.nsf.gov/statistics/srvyabs/.

(e.g., once per week, once per month, once every 6 months). Finally, as an important guide to policy, the survey could explore the pathways through which such knowledge, software, data, or other digital outputs from federal labs were acquired, including, for example, licenses, cooperative arrangements, publications, public meetings or conferences, informal information exchange, use of facilities, and hiring. Note that these pathways should not be viewed as mutually exclusive.

Survey Questions Concerning the Acquisition and Commercialization of Developed Inventions

In addition to the knowledge flows that may serve as inputs into firms' R&D, a survey could elicit data on the extent to which firms acquire and commercialize such inventions as developed ideas, software, overall concepts, and prototypes.[13] Following the methodology used by Arora and colleagues (2016), questions bearing on the acquisition and commercialization of inventions from the federal laboratories would first ask whether the firm introduced any "new" products in the prior 3 years; whether these products were new to the firm; and if so, also new to the firm's market. Then, focusing the respondent's attention on a specific, important new product (e.g., one accounting for a plurality of sales revenue in the firm's line of business), the survey could continue by asking whether that new product either was a digital one (e.g., software, data) or had an essential digital component.

Given an affirmative response to the previous question, a line of inquiry could be followed to obtain a sense of how the federal labs compare with other sources of innovation, and thus how important they are in the division of innovative labor in the U.S. economy. Questions on the source of the invention underlying the new product in question (i.e., the overall concept or prototype) would include a comprehensive range of possibilities (the firm's own R&D activities, suppliers, buyers, independent inventors, contractors, universities, the federal labs). Then, as with knowledge flows, if the firm acquired the invention from an outside source, the survey could identify the channel(s) used to acquire it (e.g., license, acquisition, contract [including software agreements], cooperative arrangement [including CRADAs], informal information exchange). In this survey, it would be critical to collect data that would allow an assessment of the importance of the new product to the firm, such as the estimated percentage of the revenue in a defined line of business accounted for by the product.

In addition to the above questions about new products (including services), the survey could inquire about the contribution of external sources, especially federal labs, to the development of new processes (i.e., new manufacturing processes, new processes for delivering services) and as sources of data and software.

---

[13] This would likely be a different survey from the one examining knowledge flows because the respondent within a firm would likely differ.

Thus in addition to collecting data on the activities and outputs of the federal labs, the committee proposes surveying firms that are potential beneficiaries of the knowledge and digital inventions produced in the labs. As noted in Chapter 6, the committee is also recommending a survey of lab managers and scientists to assess a variety of individual factors and organizational practices that may both affect the propensity of scientists to engage in technology transfer and identify best practices in managing technology transfer. Thus, the committee proposes three data collection efforts:

- data from individual federal labs on numerous dimensions of technology transfer, supplementing existing data-gathering efforts;
- data from scientists working at federal labs; and
- data from companies relating to their interactions with federal labs.

IN CLOSING

The committee recognizes that the collection of additional data from federal laboratories and companies may represent a substantial burden of time and effort. Any additional efforts to collect data from the labs and their personnel will therefore need to be appropriately resourced to ensure that the data can be gathered without compromising other lab responsibilities and without placing a burden on technology transfer offices to fund these efforts, which could incentivize them to seek to raise money through royalties and licensing. The allocation of resources will also need to take into account the training and technology needed to collect and analyze the data on the proposed new metrics. To reduce the cost and time burden, the government could, whenever possible, use public and commercially available data and new research tools to supplement or replace the proposed new survey efforts. For instance, the government could use textual analysis techniques to link data on licenses held by the government to patents, systematically track software, and identify startup activities by federal employees. The Federal Lab Consortium has contracted with the Association of University Technology Managers to improve its reporting of metrics, and this initiative holds promise for resulting in better metrics and data-collection methods. Company surveys could be made part of annual reports of licensees. The government could also consider establishing a centralized public repository of information on licenses that might assist in academic research on these topics. Unnecessary data-collection efforts or failure to leverage technological capabilities to collect data that already exist will add to the burdens placed on labs and could discourage the transfer of knowledge and technology.

FINDINGS AND RECOMMENDATIONS

Finding 7-1: Both existing metrics on federal laboratory activities that may result in the commercialization of digital products and the reporting of these metrics are inadequate. Thus, they do not allow for a comprehensive assessment of the commercialization of either digital products arising from research at federal labs or the federally developed inputs into that research, including their broader impact on the economy.

Recommendation 7-1: The Interagency Working Group on Technology Transfer and the National Science Foundation should coordinate on the collection of a more comprehensive set of metrics on both the inputs and outputs of those federal laboratory activities that may result in commercialization of digital products. These metrics should be reported in the annual report to Congress from the National Institute of Standards and Technology. These metrics should include, but not be limited to, participation in public conferences or meetings, technology transfer budgets, number of employees in the technology transfer office of each lab, research and development (R&D) budgets, the composition of R&D (e.g., percentage of effort devoted to basic research, applied research, and development), software downloads, software licenses, data downloads, cooperative arrangements, software licensing royalties, invention disclosures, patents, and copyrights. This information should be tracked annually and reported publicly at the individual lab level except where national security might be compromised.

Recommendation 7-2: The National Institute of Standards and Technology or the Office of Management and Budget should direct federal agencies to provide a more comprehensive accounting of the activities of and results produced by all cooperative research and development agreements and all other cooperative arrangements between the federal laboratories and the private sector, including accounting of failures.

Recommendation 7-3: The National Science Foundation's National Center for Science and Engineering Statistics (NCSES) should develop survey questions for firms, in accordance with Paperwork Reduction Act requirements, regarding the data, software, digital content, knowledge, and inventions originating from the federal laboratories that have contributed to firms' commercialization of new products, processes, and services. Firms should also report on the patents, processes, and products to which the outputs of the federal labs have contributed. These survey questions should encompass firms' cooperative activities with the labs and the usability of datasets and software released by the labs. These questions could be included in NCSES's Annual Business Survey or in a separate survey should NCSES conclude that this would be a more effective means of data collection.

Recommendation 7-4: Federal agencies should dedicate sufficient resources to measurement such that analysts and policy makers will have the information needed to develop recommendations regarding the federal laboratories' technology transfer and other activities that impact the commercialization of the labs' research and development outputs, including those related to digital products. To this end, the National Science Foundation should standardize the collection and reporting of the current data elements and those proposed by the committee. The Office of Management and Budget and Congress should support both the efforts of the National Center for Science and Engineering Statistics to develop and conduct these surveys and the efforts of the labs to meet these data collection requirements.

References

Adams, J. D., E. P. Chiang, and J. L. Jensen. 2003. The influence of federal laboratory R&D on industrial research. *The Review of Economics and Statistics* 85(4):1003-1020.

Allison, J. R. and L. L. Ouellette (2016). How courts adjudicate patent definiteness and disclosure. *Duke Law Journal* 65(4):609-695.

Arora, A., W. Cohen, and J. Walsh. 2016. The acquisition and commercialization of invention in American manufacturing: Incidence and impact. *Research Policy* 45:1113-1128.

Bagley, M. 2006. Academic discourse and proprietary rights: Putting patents in their proper place. *Boston College Law Review* 47(2), No. 2.

Battelle Technology Partnership Practice. 2013. The impact of genomics on the U.S. economy. https://web.ornl.gov/sci/techresources/Human_Genome/publicat/2013BattelleReportImpact-of-Genomics-on-the-US-Economy.pdf.

Belenzon, N., and M. Schankerman. 2009. University knowledge transfer: Private ownership, incentives, and local development objectives. *Journal of Law and Economics* 52(1):111-144.

Bercovitz, J., and M. Feldman. 2008. Academic entrepreneurs: Organizational change at the individual level. *Organization Science* 19:69-89.

Bercovitz, J., M. Feldman, I. Feller, and R. Burton. 2001. Organizational structure as determinants of academic patent and licensing behavior: An exploratory study of Duke, Johns Hopkins, and Pennsylvania State Universities. *Journal of Technology Transfer* 26:21-35.

Bessen, J., and M. J. Meurer. 2009. *Patent Failure: How Judges, Bureaucrats, and Lawyers Put Innovators at Risk*. Princeton, NJ: Princeton Univ. Press.

Beyer, R. A., T. Fong, M. B. Allan, J. Laura, M. P. Milazzo, R. G. Deen, and W. M. Burke. 2018. *No to NOSA, Yes to Mainstream Licenses*. Sagan Center at the SETI Institute. http://surveygizmoresponseuploads.s3.amazonaws.com/fileuploads/15647/4054745/52-84143c3de87f92bed8d9d85e21dae32f_BeyerRossEtal.pdf.

Buchanan, J. M., and Y. J. Yoon. 2000. Symmetric tragedies: Commons and anticommons. *Journal of Law and Economics* 43:1-13.

Burk, D. L., and M. A. Lemley. 2009. *The Patent Crisis and How Courts Can Solve It*. Chicago: Univ. Chicago Press.

Chander, A., and M. Sunder. 2004. *The Romance of the Public Domain*. UC Davis Law, Legal Studies Research Paper No. 13. https://ssrn.com/abstract=562301.

Chandler, J. P. 1991. Protection of U.S. competitiveness in the international software markets: Reexamining the question of copyrighting government-created software. *George Washington Journal of International Law and Economics* 25:387.

Chien, C. V., and J. Y. Wu. 2018. Decoding patentable subject matter. *Patently-O Patent Law Journal* 1.

Choi, H., H. E. Lee, D. S. Siegel, D. Waldman, and M. S. Mitchell. 2020. Assessing differences between university and federal laboratory postdoctoral scientists in technology transfer. Working Paper.

Choudhry, V., and T. A. Ponzio. 2020. Modernizing federal technology transfer metrics. *Journal of Technology Transfer* 45:544-559.

Cohen, J., and M. Lemley. 2001. Patent scope and innovation in the software industry. *California Law Review* 89:1-57.

Cohen, W. M., R. R. Nelson, and J. P. Walsh. 2002. Links and impacts: The influence of public research on industrial R&D. *Management Science* 48(1):1-23.

Cohen, W., H. Sauermann, and P. Stephan. 2020. Not in the job description: The commercial activities of academic scientists and engineers. *Management Science, INFORMS*, 66(9):4108-4117.

Colaianni, A., S. Chandrasekharan, and R. Cook-Deegan. 2010. Impact of gene patents and licensing practices on access to genetic testing and carrier screening for Tay-Sachs and Canavan disease. *Genetics in Medicine* 12(4):S5-S14.

Colyvas, J., M. Crow, A. Gelijns, R. Mazzoleni, R. R. Nelson, N. Rosenberg, and B. N. Sampat. 2002. How do university inventions get into practice? *Management Science* 48(1):61-72.

Conover, J., T. Slaper, T. Hall, and M. Kinghorn. 2010. *The Economic Contribution of the Department of the Navy Technology Transfer Program.* Bloomington: Indiana University Kelley School of Business. https://www.ibrc.indiana.edu/studies/t2.pdf.

Contigiani, A., and D. H. Hsu. 2019, January 29. How trade secrets hurt innovation. *Harvard Business Review.*

Contigiani, A., D. H. Hsu, and I. Barankay. 2018. Trade secrets and innovation: Evidence from the "inevitable disclosure" doctrine. *Strategic Management Journal* 39(11):2921-2942.

Contreras, J. L. 2011. Bermuda's legacy: Patents, policy and the design of the genome commons. *Minnesota Journal of Law, Science and Technology* 12:61.

Contreras, J. L. 2013. Confronting the crisis in scientific publishing: Latency, licensing, and access. *Santa Clara Law Review* 53:491.

Contreras, J. L. 2017. Leviathan in the commons: Biomedical data and the state. In *Governing Medical Knowledge Commons,* K. Strandburg, B. Frischmann, and M. Madison, Eds. New York: Cambridge Univ. Press.

Contreras, J. L., and B. M. Knoppers. 2018. The genomic commons. *Annual Review of Genomics and Human Genetics* 19:429-453.

Contreras, J., and J. H. Reichman. 2015. Sharing by design: Data and decentralized commons. *Science* 350(6266):1312-1314.

Cook-Deegan, R., and C. Heaney. 2010. Patents in genomics and human genetics. *Annual Review of Genomics and Human Genetics* 11:383.

Coyle, D., S. Diepeveen, J. Wdowin, L. Kay, and J. Tennison. 2020. *The Value of Data.* Bennett Institute for Public Policy, Cambridge, in partnership with the Open Data Institute. https://www.bennettinstitute.cam.ac.uk/media/uploads/files/Value_of_data_Policy_Implications_Report_26_Feb_ok4noWn.pdf.

DOD (U.S. Department of Defense). 2020. *DOD Freedom of Information Act Handbook.* https://open.defense.gov/transparency/FOIA/FOIA-handbook.

Dolmans, S. A. M., S. Shane, J. Jankowski, I. M. Reymen, and A. G. L. Romme. 2016. The evaluation of university inventions: Judging a book by its cover? *Journal of Business Research* 69(11):4998-5001.

Dratler, J. R. 1985. Trade secret law: An impediment to trade in computer software. *Santa Clara Computer and High-Technology Law Journal* 1(1):27.

Eisenberg, R. S. 1990. Patenting the human genome. *Emory Law Journal* 39:721.

Executive Office of the President. 2011. *Presidential Memorandum—Accelerating Technology Transfer and Commercialization of Federal Research in Support of High-Growth Businesses.* Washington, DC. https://obamawhitehouse.archives.gov/the-press-office/2011/10/28/presidential-memorandum-accelerating-technology-transfer-and-commerciali.

Executive Office of the President. 2013. *Patent Assertion and U.S. Innovation.* Washington, DC. https://obamawhitehouse.archives.gov/sites/default/files/docs/patent_report.pdf.

Executive Office of the President. 2018. *President's Management Agenda.* Washington, DC. https://www.whitehouse.gov/wp-content/uploads/2018/04/The PresidentsManagementAgenda.pdf.

Fagundes, D., and A. Perzanowski. 2020. Abandoning copyright. *William and Mary Law Review.* https://scholarlycommons.law.case.edu/faculty_publications/2060.

Feldman, R. 2018. Artificial intelligence: The importance of trust & distrust. *Green Bag*, 21(3).

Feldman, R., and M. A. Lemley. 2018. The sound and fury of patent activity. *Minnesota Law Review* 103:1793.

Feldman, R., B. Change Rowe, and R. Oral. 2020. Viral licensing: Ensuring the public interest when taxpayers fund pharmaceutical research. *Santa Clara Law Review* 59(3).

Former, J. 2019. Machines as the new Oompa-Loompas: Trade secrecy, the cloud, machine learning, and automation. *NYU Law Review* 94:706.

Frakes, M. D., and M. F. Wasserman. 2017. Is the time allocated to review patent applications including examiners to grant invalid patents? Evidence from microlevel application data. *The Review of Economics and Statistics* 99(3):550-563.

FSF (Free Software Foundation). 2020. *Various Licenses and Comments about Them.* https://www.gnu.org/licenses/license-list.html#NASA.

GAO (U.S. General Accounting Office). 1988. *Technology Transfer—Constraints Perceived by Federal Laboratory and Agency Officials.* Briefing Report to the Chairman, Committee on Science, Space and Technology, House of Representatives.

REFERENCES

GAO. 1990. *Technology Transfer—Copyright Law Constrains Commercialization of Some Federal Software*. Report to the Chairman, Subcommittee on Courts, Intellectual Property and the Administration of Justice, Committee on the Judiciary, House of Representatives.

GAO. 1991. *Copyright Law Constraints on the Transfer of Certain Federal Computer Software with Commercial Applications*. GAO Testimony before the U.S. Senate Committee on Commerce, Science and Transportation.

Gellman, R. M. 1994. Twin evils: Government copyright and copyright-like controls over government information. *Syracuse Law Review* 45:999.

Gingrich, N. 2018. Federal office of research and technology applications survey results. *NIST Technology Transfer Brief 1*. Gaithersburg, MD: National Institute of Standards and Technology.

Graham, S., and S. Vishnubhakat. 2013. Of smart phone wars and software patents. *Journal of Economic Perspectives* 27(1):67-86.

Ham, R. M., and D. Mowery. 1995. Improving industry-government cooperative R&D. *Issues in Science and Technology* Summer:67-73.

Heller, M. A., and R. S. Eisenberg. 1998. Can patents deter Innovation? The anti-commons in biomedical research. *Science* 280(5364):698-701.

Hemel, D., and L. L. Ouellette. 2017. Bayh-Dole beyond borders. *Journal of Law and the Biosciences* 4:282.

Hollander, A. J. 2003. Patenting computer data structures: The ghost, the machine and the federal circuit. *Duke Law & Technology Review*. https://scholarship.law.duke.edu/cgi/viewcontent.cgi?article=1102&context=dltr.

Hughes, M. E., S. V. Howieson, G. Walejko, N. Gupta, S. Jonas, A. Brenner, D. Holmes, E. Shyu, and S. Shipp. 2011. Technology transfer and commercialization landscape of the federal laboratories. *Paper NS P-4728*. Alexandria, VA: IDA/Science and Technology Institute.

IAWGTT (The Interagency Workgroup on Technology Transfer). 2012, November. *Accelerating Technology Transfer and Commercialization of Federal Research in Support of High-Growth Businesses*. Revised technology transfer metrics in response to the October 28, 2011 presidential memorandum. https://www.nist.gov/system/files/documents/2017/05/09/MetricsPaper-FINAL-1-29-13.pdf.

IITRI (Illinois Institute of Technology Research Institute). 1994. *The Congressional Ada Mandate.* http://archive.adaic.com/pol-hist/policy/mandate.txt.

IOM (Institute of Medicine). 2003. *Large-Scale Biomedical Science.* Washington, DC: National Research Council.

IOM, NASEM, and NRC (Institute of Medicine; National Academies of Sciences, Engineering, and Medicine; and National Research Council). 1995. *Allocating Federal Funds for Science and Technology.* Washington, DC: National Academies Press. https://doi.org/10.17226/5040.

Jensen, K., and F. Murray. 2005. Intellectual property landscape of the human genome. *Science* 310(5746):239-240.

Jensen, R., Thursby, J., and T. Marie. 2003. The disclosure and licensing of university inventions: The best we can do with the s**t we get to work with. *International Journal of Industrial Organization* 21(9):1271-1300.

Katyal, S. K. 2020. The paradox of source code secrecy. *Cornell Law Review* 104(1183):1194.

Keller, S., G. Korkmaz, C. Robbins, and S. Shipp. 2018. Opportunities to observe and measure intangible inputs to innovation: Definitions, operationalization, and examples. *Proceedings of the National Academy of Sciences* 115(50):12638-12645.

Lach, S., and M. Schankerman. 2004. Royalty sharing and technology licensing in universities. *Journal of the European Economic Association* 2:252-264.

Lally, B. 2019, December 5. Presentation to National Academies Committee on Accelerating Commercialization at the Federal Laboratories. Washington, DC.

Lemley, M. A. 2011. The surprising virtues of treating trade secrets as IP rights. In *The Law and Theory of Trade Secrecy: A Handbook of Contemporary Research*, R. C. Dreyfuss and K. J. Strandburg, Eds. Cheltenham, UK: Edward Elgar, p. 109.

Lemley, M. A. 2013. Software patents and the return of functional claiming. *Wisconsin Law Review* 905.

Levine, D. S. 2011. The impact of trade secrecy on public transparency. In *The Law and Theory of Trade Secrecy: A Handbook of Contemporary Research* (), R. C. Dreyfuss and K. J. Strandburg, Eds. Cheltenham, UK: Edward Elgar, p. 406.

Link, A. N., and D. S. Siegel. 2005. Generating science-based growth: An econometric analysis of the impact of organizational incentives on university-industry technology transfer. *European Journal of Finance* 11:169-182.

Link, A. N., Z. T. Oliver, G. B. Jordan, and C. Hayter. 2019. *Overview and Analysis of Technology Transfer from Federal Agencies and Laboratories.* RTI Project Number 0214999. RTI International.

Marx, M., and L. Fleming. 2020. Non-compete agreements: Barriers to entry . . . and exit? *Innovation Policy and the Economy* 20.

Milgrim, R. M., and E. E. Benson. n.d. *Milgrim on Trade Secrets.* New York: Matthew Bender Elite Products.

Miller, A. R. 1993. Copyright protection for computer programs, databases, and computer-generated works: Is anything new since CONTU? *Harvard Law Review* 106:97.

Miller, H. M., L. Richardson, and S. R. Koontz, J. Loomis, and L. Koontz. 2013. Users, uses, and value of Landsat satellite imagery—Results from the 2012 survey of users. *U.S. Geological Survey Open-File Report* 1269:51. http://dx.doi.org/10.3133/ofr20131269.

Millien, R. 2020, February 17. Six years after Alice: 61.8% of U.S. patents issued in 2019 were "software-related"—Up 21.6% from 2018. *IP Watchdog.* https://www.ipwatchdog.com/2020/02/17/six-years-alice-61-8-u-s-patents-issued-2019-software-related-21-6-2018/id=118986.

Mossinghoff, G. J., and R. F. Allnutt. 1967. Patent infringement in government procurement: A remedy without a right. *Notre Dame Law Review* 42(1).

Mowery, D. C. 2003. Using cooperative research and development agreements as S&T indicators: What do we have and what would we like? *Technology Analysis and Strategic Management*, 15:189-205.

Mowery, D. C., R. R. Nelson, B. Sampat, and A. A. Ziedonis. 2001. The growth of patenting and licensing by U.S. universities: An Assessment of the effects of the Bayh–Dole Act of 1980. *Research Policy*, 30:99-119.

MPEP (*Manual of Patent Examining Procedure*). n.d. https://www.bitlaw.com/source/mpep/608_05.html.

Murphy, K. 2019, December 5. Presentation to National Academies Committee on Accelerating Commercialization at the Federal Laboratories. Washington, DC.

Nagaraj, A. 2018, October 22. *The Private Impact of Public Information: Landsat Satellite Maps and Gold Exploration.* https://abhishekn.com/files/nagaraj_landsat_oct2018.pdf.

NASEM (National Academies of Sciences, Engineering, and Medicine). 2018. *Open Source Software Policy Options for NASA Earth and Space Sciences.* Washington, DC: The National Academies Press.

NHGRI (National Human Genome Research Institute). 1996. *NHGRI Policy Regarding Intellectual Property of Human Genomic Sequence.* Bethesda, MD: National Institutes of Health.

NIH (National Institutes of Health). 2005, April 11. Best Practices for the Licensing of Genomic Inventions: Final Notice, 70 *Federal Register* 70(68):18413.

Nimmer, D. (n.d.) 1 *Nimmer on Copyright.* New York: Matthew Bender Elite Products.

Nimmer, D. (n.d.) 4 *Nimmer on Copyright.* New York: Matthew Bender Elite Products.

NIST (National Institute of Standards and Technology). 2019a. *Federal Laboratory Technology Transfer Fiscal Year 2016: Summary Report to the President and the Congress.* Washington, DC: U.S. Department of Commerce. https://www.nist.gov/system/files/documents/2019/10/30/fy2016_fed_lab_tech_transfer_rept_fina_9-10-19.pdf.

NIST. 2019b. *NIST Special Publication 1234: Return on Investment Initiative for Unleashing American Innovation.* Washington, DC: U.S. Department of Commerce. https://doi.org/10.6028/NIST.SP.1234.

Nodiff, M. J. 1984. Copyrightability of works of the federal and state governments under the 1976 Act. *Saint Louis University Law Journal* 29:91.

NRC (National Research Council). 2006. *Reaping the Benefits of Genomic and Proteomic Research.* Washington, DC: National Academies Press.

NRC. 2011. *Managing University Intellectual Property in the Public Interest.* Washington, DC: The National Academies Press. https://doi.org/10.17226/13001.

NSB and NSF (National Science Board and National Science Foundation). 2020. *Science and Engineering Indicators 2020: The State of U.S. Science and Engineering.* Alexandria, VA: National Science Foundation, Figure 28. https://ncses.nsf.gov/pubs/nsb20201.

REFERENCES

O'Connor, A. C., M. P. Gallaher, K. Clark-Sutton, D. Lapidus, Z. T. Oliver, T. J. Scott, D. W. Wood, M. A. Gonzalez, E. G. Brown, and J. Fletcher. 2019. *Economic Benefits of the Global Positioning System (GPS)*. RTI Report No. 0215471. Research Triangle Park, NC: RTI International.

Okediji, R. L. 2016. Government as owner of intellectual property: Considerations for public welfare in an era of big data. *Vanderbilt Journal of Entertainment and Technology Law* 18:331.

OSTP (Office of Science and Technology Policy). 2020, March 23. *White House Announces New Partnership to Unleash U.S. Supercomputing Resources to Fight COVID-19.* https://www.whitehouse.gov/briefings-statements/white-house-announces-new-partnership-unleash-u-s-supercomputing-resources-fight-covid-19.

Powell, W. W., and J. Owen-Smith. 1998. Universities and the market for intellectual property in the life sciences. *Journal of Policy Analysis and Management* 17(2):253-277.

Price, S., and D. S. Siegel. 2019. Assessing the role of the federal government in the development of new products, industries, and companies: Case study evidence since World War II. *Annals of Science and Technology Policy* 3(4). DOI: 10.1561/110.00000016.

Rai, A. K. 2012. Patent validity across the executive branch: Ex ante foundations for policy development. *Duke Law Journal* 61:1237.

Rai, A. K., and R. S. Eisenberg. 2003. Bayh-Dole reform and the progress of biomedicine. *Law and Contemporary Problems* 66:289.

Rai, A., J. Allison, and B. Sampat. 2009. University software ownership and litigation: A first examination. *North Carolina Law Review* 87:1519-1570.

Raymond, E. S. 1999. *The Cathedral and the Bazaar: Musings on Linux and Open Source by an Accidental Revolutionary*. Sebastopol, CA: O'Reilly and Associates, Inc. (Revised 2001).

Reichman, J. H., and P. F. Uhlir. 2003. A contractually reconstructed research commons for scientific data in a highly protectionist intellectual property environment. *Law and Contemporary Problems* 66:315.

Reilly, S., and S. Waxman. 2016. Licensing technology developed with public funds. *Landslide* 9(2):42-47.

Reinecke, J. D. 2019. Is the Supreme Court's patentable subject matter test overly ambiguous: An empirical test. *Utah Law Review* 2019:581.

Saltiel, J. 2019, August. In the courts: Five years after Alice—Five lessons learned from the treatment of software patents in litigation. *WIPO Magazine.*

Samuelson, P. 1984. CONTU revisited: The case against copyright protection for computer programs in machine-readable form. *Duke Law Journal* 663.

Sapienza, H. J., and M. A. Korsgaard. 1996. Procedural justice in entrepreneur-investor relations. *Academy of Management Journal*, 39:544-574.

Sapienza, H. J., M. A. Korsgaard, P. K. Goulet, and J. P. Hoogendam. 2000. Effects of agency risks and procedural justice on board processes in venture capital-backed firms. *Entrepreneurship & Regional Development*, 12: 331–351.

Shane, S., S. A. M. Dolmans, J. Jankowski, I. M. M. J. Reymen, and A. G. L. Romme. 2015. "Academic entrepreneurship: Which inventors do technology licensing officers prefer for spinoffs?" The Journal of Technology Transfer 40(2):273–292.

Sichelman, T. 2010. Commercializing patents. *Stanford Law Review* 59(1).

Snyder, B., and J. W. Thomas. 2014. *GOGOs, GOCOs, and FFRDCs...Oh My!* Chicago, IL: Federal Laboratory Consortium for Technology Transfer.

Stevens, A., G. Johnson, and P. Sanberg. 2011. The role of patents and commercialization in the tenure and promotion process. *Technology & Innovation* 13(3).

Straub, C. L., S. R. Koontz, and J. B. Loomis. 2019. *Economic Valuation of Landsat Imagery: U.S. Geological Survey Open-File Report 2019–1112.* https://doi.org/10.3133/ofr20191112.

Thomas, J. R. 2014. *The Role of Trade Secrets in Innovation Policy.* Congressional Research Service Report. https://fas.org/sgp/crs/secrecy/R41391.pdf.

Thursby, J. G., and M. C. Thursby. (2007). University licensing. *Oxford Review of Economic Policy* 23(4):620-639.

Trajtenberg, M. 1990. A penny for your quotes: Patent citations and the value of innovations. *RAND Journal of Economics* 21(1), Spring.

Tran, J. L. 2016. Two years after *Alice v. CLS Bank. Journal of the Patent and Trademark Office Society* 98:354.

Tran, J. L., and J. S. Benevento. 2019. Alice at five. *Patently-O Patent Law Journal* 25.

REFERENCES

Tripp, S., and M. Grueber. 2013. *Economic Impact of the Human Genome Project*. Battelle Memorial Institute. http://www.battelle.org/docs/default-document-library/economic_impact_of_the_human_genome_project.pdf?sfvrsn=2.

U.S. Copyright Office. 2017. *Compendium of U.S. Copyright Office Practices*. § 721; 721.5.

U.S. House of Representatives. 1976, September 3. *Copyright Law Revision*. Report No. 94-1476.

U.S. House of Representatives Subcommittee on Intellectual Property and Judicial Administration of the Committee on the Judiciary. 1992. Hearings on H.R. 191, Technology Transfer Improvements Act of 1991 (including Statement of Assistant Secretary of Commerce for Technology Policy Deborah Wince-Smith).

U.S. Senate. 1975, November 20. *Copyright Law Revision* Report No. 94-473.

Veletsianos, G., and R. Kimmons. 2012. Assumptions and challenges of open scholarship. *The International Review of Research in Open and Distributed Learning* 13(4):166. DOI: 10.19173/irrodl.v13i4.1313.

Williams, H. L. 2013. Intellectual property rights and innovation: Evidence from the human genome. *Journal of Political Economy* 121(1).

Willinksy, J. 2006. *The Access Principle: The Case for Open Access to Research and Scholarship*. Cambridge, MA: MIT Press.

Zucker, L., and M. Darby. 2001. Capturing technological opportunity via Japan's star scientists: Evidence from Japanese firms' biotech patents and products. *Journal of Technology Transfer* 26(1).

APPENDIXES

Appendix A

Agendas

FIRST MEETING: SEPTEMEBER 5-6, 2019

Thursday—September 5, 2019
Keck Center of the National Academies of Sciences, Engineering, and Medicine

CLOSED SESSION (9:00 AM–11:00 AM)

OPEN SESSION (11:00 AM–12:00 PM)

11:00 AM **Agency Perspectives (I)**
What are the U.S. government's goals and expectations for the study? What data can the government make available for committee use?
Jennifer Shieh, White House Office of Science and Technology Policy

12:00 PM **Return to Closed Session**

CLOSED SESSION (12:00 PM–1:30 PM)

OPEN SESSION (1:30 PM–2:30 PM)

1:30 PM   **Agency Perspectives (II)**
               What are the U.S. government's goals and expectations for the study? What data can the government make available for committee use?
               Courtney Silverthorn, National Institute of Standards and Technology

2:30 PM   **Break; Return to Closed Session**

CLOSED SESSION (2:45 PM–5:30 PM)

Friday—September 6, 2019
Keck Center of the National Academies of Sciences, Engineering, and Medicine

CLOSED SESSION (9:00 AM–1:00 PM)

SECOND MEETING: DECEMBER 5-6, 2019

Thursday—December 5, 2019
Duke Center, Washington, DC

CLOSED SESSION (8:15 AM–9:00 AM)

OPEN SESSION (9:00 AM–4:15 PM)

9:00 AM   **Welcome and Introductions**
               Ruth Okediji, Harvard University, and Donald Siegel, Arizona State University (Committee Co-chairs)

9:10 AM   **Panel I: Overview of Technology Transfer at DOE and NASA**
               Moderator: Jetta Wong, JLW Advising (Committee Member)

APPENDIX A

Panels I and II will address the types of digital products created at federal laboratories, technology transfer and commercialization of these digital products, considerations in determining how to optimize use of these digital products, including whether to use open access, open source or proprietary dissemination methods, and barriers to technology transfer.

> John LaBarge, *Office of Laboratory Policy, Office of Science, Department of Energy*, and Brian Lally, *Office of General Counsel, Department of Energy*
> Robert Leland, *National Renewable Energy Laboratory*
> Don Macdonald, *Office of Technology Transitions, Department of Energy*
> Kevin Murphy, *NASA*

11:00 AM **Break**

11:15 AM **Panel II: Overview of Technology Transfer at NASA (continued), DOD and NIH**
Moderator: Margo Bagley, Emory University (Committee Member)

> Thomas Huang, *Strategic Lead for Interactive Analytics, Jet Propulsion Lab*
> Jordan Kasper, *Defense Digital Service*
> Bernadette Johnson, *Technology Ventures Office, Lincoln Labs*
> Mark Rohrbaugh, *Office of the Director, National Institutes of Health*, and Andrea Jackson-Dipina, *Office of Science Policy, National Institutes of Health*

1:15 PM **Working Lunch**
John Dement, *Chair, Federal Laboratory Consortium, and Crane Division, Naval Surface Warfare Center, Department of Defense*

2:00 PM **Panel III: Assessing the Value of Digital Products from Federal Laboratories**

This panel will discuss methods for assessing the value of digital products.

Moderator: Joel Waldfogel, University of Minnesota (Committee Member)

Assessing the Value of Open Source Software
Stephanie Shipp, University of Virginia

Private Use of Public Information
Abhishek Nagaraj, University of California, Berkeley

Assessing the Value of Publications
Cassidy Sugimoto, National Science Foundation

3:30 PM **Break**

3:45 PM **Research on Industrial Use of Public R&D Research**
Wes Cohen, Duke University and NBER (Committee Member)

4:15 PM **Return to Closed Session**

CLOSED SESSION (4:15 PM–4:45 PM)

Friday—December 6, 2019
National Academy of Sciences

CLOSED SESSION (8:00 AM–9:00 AM)

OPEN SESSION (9:00 AM–11:00 AM)

9:00 AM **Welcome and Introductions**
Ruth Okediji, Harvard University, and Donald Siegel, Arizona State University (Committee Co-chairs)

9:10 AM **Panel IV: Intermediary and Industry Partnerships with Labs**
Moderator: Arti Rai, Duke University (Committee Member)

This session will highlight successful laboratory partnerships and barriers.

Ilan Gur, Activate (via video)
Jonathan Bryce, OpenStack Foundation

APPENDIX A

>   *Darin Oelkers, TechLink*
>   *Art Koehler, Procter and Gamble*
>   *Christopher O'Neill, IBM Corporation (via video)*
>   *Jennifer Garson, Office of Energy Efficiency and Renewable Energy, Department of Energy*

11:00 AM   Return to Closed Session

CLOSED SESSION (11:00 AM–1:00 PM)

THIRD MEETING: JANUARY 30, 2020

Thursday—January 30, 2020
Keck Center of the National Academies of Sciences, Engineering, and Medicine

OPEN SESSION (12:00 PM–1:30 PM)

12:00 PM   **Welcome and Introductions**
                Ruth Okediji, Harvard University, and Donald Siegel, Arizona State University (Committee Co-chairs) (via Zoom)

12:05 PM   **Panel Discussion: Tech Transfer of Digital Products at DOE Labs**

>   *Lee Cheatham, Director, Technology Deployment and Outreach, Pacific Northwest National Laboratory (PNNL), and Chair, National Lab Technology Transfer Group (NLTT) executive committee* (via Zoom)
>   *Jason Stolworthy, Director, Technology Deployment, Idaho National Laboratory (INL); and Vice Chair, National Lab Technology Transfer Group (NLTT) executive committee* (via Zoom)
>   *Richard Rankin, Director, Innovation & Partnerships Office, Lawrence Livermore National Laboratory (LLNL), and immediate Past Chair, National Lab Technology Transfer Group (NLTT) executive committee* (via Zoom)

1:30 PM   **Adjourn**

FOURTH MEETING: MARCH 2-3, 2020

Monday—March 2, 2020
Keck Center of the National Academies of Sciences, Engineering, and Medicine

OPEN SESSION (9:00 AM–12:45 PM)

9:00 AM   **Welcome and Introductions**
Ruth Okediji, Harvard University, and Donald Siegel, Arizona State University (Committee Co-chairs)

9:05 AM   **Panel I: Intellectual Property Issues Related to Digital Products from Federal Labs**
Moderator: Margo Bagley, Emory University (Committee Member)

John Karasek, Supervisory Intellectual Property Counsel, ONR, Section 801 Licensing Authority for Software
Bryan Geurts, Senior IP Counsel, NASA Goddard Space Center
Hope O'Keeffe, Senior Associate General Counsel, Library of Congress
Michael Carroll, Professor of Intellectual Property, American University Law School

10:45 AM   **Break**

11:00 AM   **Panel II: Developing the Digital World**
Moderator: Mary Beth Campbell, California Institute of Technology (Committee Member)

Shane Greenstein, Professor, Harvard University Business School
Katherine Strandburg, Law Professor, New York University Law School (via Zoom)
Drew Bennett, Associate Director, Software Licensing, Technology Transfer Office, University of Michigan
Mary Monson and Robert Westervelt, Office of Technology Transfer, Sandia National Laboratory (via Zoom)

APPENDIX A

12:20 PM   **Management of Conflict of Interest**
                Brian Lally, Office of General Counsel, Department of Energy

12:45 PM   **Break; Go to Closed Session**

CLOSED SESSION (1:00 PM–5:30 PM)

Tuesday—March 3, 2020
Keck Center of the National Academies of Sciences, Engineering, and Medicine

CLOSED SESSION (9:00 AM–1:00 PM)

FIFTH MEETING: MAY 26, 2020

Tuesday—May 26, 2020
via Zoom

OPEN SESSION (11:30 AM–12:45 PM)

11:30 AM   **Welcome and Introductions**
                Ruth Okediji, Harvard University, and Donald Siegel, Arizona State University (Committee Co-chairs)

11:35 AM   **Panel Discussion: Tech Transfer of Digital Products at Federal Labs**
                Adam Cohen, President and CEO, Associated Universities, Inc. (AUI)
                Barry Costa, Director of Strategic Partnerships and Licensing, MITRE
                Daniel Broderick, Manager, Office of Technology Transfer, Jet Propulsion Laboratory (JPL)
                Eric Payne, Senior Licensing Executive, and Anne Miller, Laboratory Technology Transfer Director, National Renewable Energy Laboratory (NREL)

12:45 PM   **Adjourn**

SIXTH MEETING: JUNE 2, 2020

Tuesday—June 2, 2020
via Zoom

CLOSED SESSION (10:30 AM–12:30 PM)

Appendix B

Biographies of Committee Members

RUTH L. OKEDIJI (CO-CHAIR)

Ruth L. Okediji is Jeremiah Smith Jr. professor of law at Harvard Law School and co-director of Harvard University's Berkman Klein Center for Internet & Society. She is an expert in intellectual property law, innovation policy, and digital copyright. A foremost authority on the role of intellectual property in economic development, Professor Okediji has advised intergovernmental organizations, regional economic communities, and national governments on the effect of global intellectual property rules on innovation policy and social welfare. She served on the National Academies' Committee on the Impact of Copyright Policy on Innovation in the Digital Era (2010–2013). Professor Okediji is a graduate of the University of Jos and Harvard Law School.

DONALD SIEGEL (CO-CHAIR)

Donald Siegel is Foundation Professor of Public Policy and Management and director of the School of Public Affairs at Arizona State University. He has written extensively on the managerial and public policy implications of technology transfer and academic entrepreneurship and has served as an editor of the *Journal of Technology Transfer* since 2002. From 2008 to 2016, he was dean of the School of Business at the University at Albany. Dr. Siegel previously chaired the National Academies' Committee on Best Practice in National Innovation Programs from Flexible Electronics (2010–2014) and was a member of the Committee on Capitalizing on Science, Technology, and Innovation from 2009 to 2016. In 2016, he was elected a fellow of the Academy of Management (AOM) and in 2020 was elected dean of the AOM fellows. Dr. Siegel holds a bachelor's degree in economics and master's and doctoral degrees in business economics from Columbia University.

MARGO A. BAGLEY

Margo A. Bagley is Asa Griggs Candler professor of law at Emory University School of Law. She rejoined the Emory faculty in 2016 after a decade at the University of Virginia School of Law, where she was most recently Hardy Cross Dillard professor of law. Her scholarship focus includes issues relating to patents, biotechnology, and technology transfer. Professor Bagley helped develop Technological Innovation: Generating Economic Results (TI:GER), a technology commercialization education program, which is a collaboration between Emory University and the Georgia Institute of Technology. She served on the National Academies' Committee on University Management of Intellectual Property: Lessons from a Generation of Experience, Research, and Dialogue (2008–2011), as well as on the United Nations Convention on Biological Diversity's Ad Hoc Technical Expert Group on Digital Sequence Information on Genetic Resources (2018). She holds a B.S. in chemical engineering from the University of Wisconsin-Madison and worked in research and development for both the Procter & Gamble Company and the Coca-Cola Company. She is a co-inventor on a U.S. patent for reduced-fat peanut butter and also held research internships at Oak Ridge National Laboratory, Lawrence Livermore National Laboratory, AT&T Bell Laboratories, and the NASA (National Aeronautics and Space Administration) Marshall Space Flight Center. She practiced law with Finnegan, Henderson, Farabow, Garrett & Dunner, LLP; and Smith, Gambrell & Russell, LLP. Professor Bagley received a J.D. in 1996 from Emory University, where she was a Robert W. Woodruff fellow and was elected to the Order of the Coif.

MARY BETH CAMPBELL

Mary Beth Campbell is director of corporate partnerships at Caltech's Office of Technology Transfer and Corporate Partnerships, where she is responsible for developing and implementing Caltech's industry engagement and research partnership strategies. At Caltech, she has worked with inventors to understand and evaluate the commercial potential of inventions; she has also participated in patent decisions, and formulated and negotiated license agreements with startups and established companies. Prior to joining Caltech, Dr. Campbell was a research staff member at the Science and Technology Policy Institute, where she managed a team of researchers studying technology transfer practices at U.S. federal laboratories. Their findings were used to inform policy decisions by federal interagency working groups and informed the October 2011 presidential memorandum "Accelerating Technology Transfer and Commercialization of Federal Research in Support of High-Growth Businesses." Prior to working at the institute, Dr. Campbell was a senior acquisition analyst with the Department of Defense and participated in the creation of a small office to perform analyses around portfolio management, competition within the defense industrial base, and metrics development. Dr. Campbell holds a Ph.D. in applied physics from Harvard University.

WESLEY M. COHEN

Wesley M. Cohen is professor of economics and management and Snow Family professor of business administration in the Fuqua School of Business at Duke University. He also holds secondary appointments in Duke's Department of Economics and School of Law, is a research associate of the National Bureau of Economic Research, and is founding faculty director of the Fuqua School's Center for Entrepreneurship and Innovation. With a research focus on the economics of technological change and research and development, Dr. Cohen has examined the determinants of innovative activity and performance, considering the roles of firm size; market structure; firm learning; knowledge flows; university research; and the means that firms use to protect their intellectual property, with a particular focus on patents. He served on the National Academies' Committee on Management of University Intellectual Property (2008–2011), Panel to Review Research and Development Statistics at the National Science Foundation (2003–2004), and Committee on Intellectual Property Rights in the Knowledge-Based Economy (2000–2004). Dr. Cohen is a magna cum laude graduate of Yale University and holds a Ph.D. in economics, also from Yale University.

MARK S. KAMLET

Mark S. Kamlet is university professor of economics and public policy and provost emeritus at Carnegie Mellon University, with joint appointments in the Department of Social and Decision Sciences in the Dietrich College of Humanities and Social Sciences and the Heinz College of Information Systems and Public Policy. He has served on the National Academies' Committee on Poison Prevention and Control, 2003–2004; Board on Population Health and Public Health Practice, 2002–2006; and Committee on Management of University Intellectual Property, 2008–2011. Dr. Kamlet is an elected fellow of the American Association for the Advancement of Science. He earned a bachelor's degree in mathematics from Stanford University and holds master's degrees in mathematical statistics and economics, and a Ph.D. in economics from the University of California, Berkeley.

ARTI RAI

Arti Rai, Elvin R. Latty professor of law and the founding faculty director of the Center for Innovation Policy at Duke University School of Law, is an internationally recognized expert in intellectual property law, innovation policy, administrative law, and health law. Her current research focuses on incentives and pricing in life sciences innovation. From 2009 to 2010, Professor Rai led the Office of Policy and International Affairs at the U.S. Patent and Trademark Office. She has also served on the National Academies' Committee on Understanding the Global Public Health Implications of Substandard, Falsified, and Counterfeit Medical Products (2012–2013) and Committee on

Strategies for Responsible Sharing of Clinical Trial Data (2013–2015), in addition to reviewing reports for other committees. Professor Rai graduated from Harvard College, magna cum laude, with a degree in biochemistry and history (history and science); attended Harvard Medical School for the 1987–1988 academic year; and earned a J.D., cum laude, from Harvard Law School in 1991.

JOEL WALDFOGEL

Joel Waldfogel is associate dean of M.B.A. and M.S. programs and Frederick R. Kappel chair in applied economics, strategic management, and entrepreneurship at the Carlson School of Management of the University of Minnesota; an affiliated faculty member in the economics department and the law school; and a research associate of the National Bureau of Economic Research. His main research interests are industrial organization and law and economics, and he has conducted empirical studies of price advertising; media markets; the operation of differentiated product markets; and issues related to digital products, including piracy, pricing, revenue sharing, and the value of new products. Dr. Waldfogel previously served on the National Academies' Committee to Improve Research Information and Data on Firearms (2001–2005) and Committee on the Impact of Copyright Policy on Innovation in the Digital Era (2010–2013). He holds a B.A. in economics from Brandeis University and a Ph.D. in economics from Stanford University.

JOHN WILBANKS

John T. Wilbanks is chief commons officer at Sage Bionetworks, where he promotes the use of technology to pool medical data, creating a commons where information is integrated and accessible. He is also a senior fellow at FasterCures and founder at Consent to Research. Mr. Wilbanks cofounded the Access to Research campaign, which resulted in increased accessibility to results of federally funded scientific research, and he started a bioinformatics company called Incellico, which became a part of Selventa in 2003. He served as a senior fellow at the Ewing Marion Kauffman Foundation and was a senior advisor for big data to the National Coordination Office. Mr. Wilbanks has past affiliations with the Massachusetts Institute of Technology's Project on Mathematics and Computation, which hosts Creative Commons, a nonprofit organization that enables knowledge sharing through free legal tools. He has also worked with Harvard University's Berkman Klein Center for Internet & Society, the World Wide Web Consortium, the U.S. House of Representatives, and Creative Commons. Mr. Wilbanks holds a B.A. in philosophy from Tulane University and studied modern letters at the Sorbonne.

JETTA WONG

Jetta Wong is president of JLW Advising, where she advises clients on how to bring new clean-energy technologies to the market. She works with laboratories, universities, and other innovation organizations to develop policies and programs focused on U.S. competitiveness and the commercialization of technologies that reduce carbon emissions. Ms. Wong is also a senior fellow in the Clean Energy Innovation Policy Program for the Information Technology & Innovation Foundation. From 2012 to 2016, she worked at the U.S. Department of Energy (DOE), where she established and served as the first director of the Office of Technology Transitions (OTT). Before her work with OTT, Ms. Wong served in the Office of Energy Efficiency and Renewable Energy, where she worked on clean energy manufacturing and led the office's National Laboratory Impact Initiative. While at DOE, she co-chaired the White House National Science and Technology Council's Lab-to-Market initiative, focused on creating economic impact from federally funded research and development. Ms. Wong has also worked for the U.S. House of Representatives' Committee on Science, Space, and Technology, where she helped establish and oversee energy and environment programs of the federal government. Prior to working for Congress, she worked for the Clean Energy Program of the Union of Concerned Scientists and the Environmental and Energy Study Institute. Ms. Wong's career in energy started in Uzbekistan, where she was a natural resources consultant on an anaerobic digestion development project. Ms. Wong holds a B.S. in natural resources and the environment from the University of Michigan and an M.P.S. in legislative affairs from The George Washington University.

Appendix C

Definitions of Digital Products

DATA

Data are digital objects broadly defined as observations or measurements (processed or unprocessed) collected in the course of scientific investigations. Data may take many forms, including numbers, text, images, and videos. Data produced by federal laboratories often have unique qualities, such as being generated by a unique piece of scientific equipment (e.g., colliders) or in massive quantities not available elsewhere (e.g., satellite data). Because of their unique and often irreplaceable qualities, these types of raw data are generally retained for archival purposes. When stored in a form amenable to external analysis, raw and/or preprocessed data may be distributed outside of the lab to ensure reproducibility of scientific results and allow external researchers to advance new use cases and improve data processing pipelines.

Datasets and Databases

While raw data may sometimes be valuable to researchers outside of the federal laboratories, it is often more beneficial for the labs to release *datasets*: structured collections of data pertaining to a particular endeavor or measurement. Like data, datasets make take many forms, including tables of numeric values, collections of images or videos, or digital formats. Datasets also can include engineering studies, such as characterization of materials, performance measurements of software systems, and failure rates for different devices.

Especially in the latter case, it may be useful to house datasets within a *database*. A database is a collection of datasets that includes a software framework that allows those datasets to be electronically accessed, analyzed, manipulated, and updated. Databases may enable not just data access but *efficient* data access, for example, by allowing access to manageable parts of datasets that are too large to retrieve using traditional techniques.

Metadata and Data Curation

Particularly when releasing data to people who have not been involved in the data's creation, it is helpful to include *metadata*—information on the structure and provenance of a dataset. Metadata, increasingly considered a digital product on its own, is often essential to locating and retrieving datasets of interest, understanding the context in which the data were produced, and making appropriate use of the data. Accurate and informative metadata is critical to good *data curation*—the process of managing datasets and the corresponding metadata to ensure that no information about the structure, provenance, or quality of data is lost. Good data curation, in turn, is an essential component of open and shareable data.

SOFTWARE

Data can often be of limited use in their raw form. *Algorithms* are computational procedures that take data as inputs and calculate outputs that answer questions and solve problems. *Software* is a human- and machine-readable set of instructions that implement an algorithm or set of algorithms. Software can be packaged for wider use as an *application* or *app*, allowing users to make use of the functionality of a piece of software without having expertise in the underlying code powering the app.

Code Snippets

Code snippets are small subsets of software with lightweight documentation intended to be reused. They allow a programmer to use a standard implementation of a specific statistical technique, reducing error and increasing replicability. Snippets are broadly available online under open-source licenses and are often deeply woven into scientific software.

Scientific Software Artifacts

A particularly important type of code snippet is a *scientific software artifact*. Such artifacts, which may take the form of data readers or calibration routines, are often an integral part of data, such that they are needed to understand the context of the data. When data are shared, the inclusion of scientific software artifacts greatly increases the usability and portability of the shared data.

STATISTICAL MODELS

Statistical models are a type of digital product that bring together data and software to enable prediction. They are a mathematical framework for predicting the outcome of empirical phenomena based on underlying parameters. Software can be used to define these models and optimize the value of their

APPENDIX C

underlying parameters based on input data. A model with optimized parameters is known as a "fitted" model, and can be used for making predictions.

Artificial Intelligence/Machine Learning (AI/ML)

AI/ML is an increasingly popular subfield of statistical modeling. AI/ML employs highly flexible models that can identify complex or unexpected patterns in data, thereby fueling increased predictive performance, instead of prescribing a specific mathematical description of a phenomenon, such as is done in traditional statistical modeling. *Deep learning*, one popular subtype of AI/ML, uses *neural networks* to "understand" very complex data, including images, text, speech, and videos.

Training Datasets

The datasets used to "fit" or "train" AI/ML models are known as *training datasets*. These large datasets often consist of many pairs of inputs and outputs (e.g., input images together with a label indicating the presence or absence of a face), and in the training process, model parameters are optimized to provide the correct output in response to a given input. It is important to provide training datasets that are both large and unbiased (as representative as possible of the full range of inputs that the model may encounter).

Software Notebooks

Software notebooks are web-based tools that support all aspects of data transformation, including workflows, code, data, equations, and visualizations. They are both human- and machine-readable, and can serve as a form of publication as well as a form of software since instructions can be executed within the document. Notebooks can live online as self-contained toolkits or as documentation of a specific data analysis and modeling attempt.[1] They can also link to other kinds of digital products, including datasets, external software, workflows, publications, and patents.[2]

---

[1] An empirical study of references to notebooks in astronomy over a 5-year period (2014–2018) found that notebooks appear better suited to supporting reuse of machine learning products than to providing direct access to software code and data. The study authors further recommend that any notebooks cited in publications be "stabilized"—frozen in time so the next user can start from the same place where the conclusions claimed were drawn. Indeed, these notebooks even serve as a discovery mechanism for reuse. Wofford, M., B. Boscoe, C. Borgman, I. Pasquetto, and M. Golshan, Milena. 2020. Jupyter notebooks as discovery mechanisms for open science: Citation practices in the astronomy community. *Computing in Science & Engineering* 22(1).

[2] Influenced by and derived from Randles, Bernadette M., et al. 2017. Using the Jupyter notebook as a tool for open science: An empirical study. *2017 ACM/IEEE Joint Conference on Digital Libraries (JCDL)*. IEEE.

OTHER DIGITAL PRODUCTS

Electronic Media

Many documents and other materials that were previously disseminated through print or other analog media are now distributed by federal laboratories in digital form. These include electronic versions of scientific publications (one vehicle for communicating scientific discoveries from federal labs); electronic manufacturing designs of physical objects; and digital images and videos for directly communicating results to the scientific community, policy makers, the media, and the general public.

Digital Services

Many scientific analyses and digital products developed at federal laboratories require more computational power than is available in a single computer. Cloud computing allows individual users to remotely access the computational power of many computers at once, which can be essential to harness and analyze the vast datasets, complex software, and powerful statistical models routinely produced by federal labs and the private sector. Computing power may be provided by a cluster of computers at an individual lab or a centralized scientific computing facility (e.g., the National Energy Research Supercomputing Center). These facilities, along with the substantial in-house computer processing and analytical expertise at federal labs, can be made available to external researchers.

In addition, federal labs support a wide range of other public-facing digital services, including time.gov (through which the National Institute of Standards and Technology [NIST] provides digital access to the official time) and weather.gov (through which the National Weather Service provides digital access to weather data). Federal labs also maintain an array of software repositories through which they can provide public access to software and code produced in the lab (e.g. osti.gov/doecode, code.mil, code.nasa.gov, software.nasa.gov, and code.nsa.gov).

Appendix D

List of Federal Laboratories

TABLE D-1 List of Federal Laboratories

Agency	Name	City	State	Type	Focus
Dept. of Agriculture (USDA)	National Agricultural Statistics Service	Washington	DC	GOGO	Environmental
Dept. of Agriculture (USDA)	U.S. Forest Service (FS)—Forest Products Laboratory (FPL)	Washington	DC	GOGO	Environmental
Dept. of Agriculture (USDA)	U.S. Forest Service (FS)—Missoula Technology and Development Center (MTDC)	Missoula	MT	GOGO	Environmental
Dept. of Agriculture (USDA)	U.S. Forest Service (FS)—Northern Research Station (NRS)	Newtown Square	PA	GOGO	Environmental
Dept. of Agriculture (USDA)	U.S. Forest Service (FS)—Pacific Northwest Research Station (PNW)	Portland	OR	GOGO	Environmental
Dept. of Agriculture (USDA)	U.S. Forest Service (FS)—Rocky Mountain Research Station (RMRS)	Fort Collins	CO	GOGO	Environmental
Dept. of Agriculture (USDA)	U.S. Forest Service (FS)—San Dimas Technology and Development Center (SDTDC)	San Dimas	CA	GOGO	Environmental
Dept. of Agriculture (USDA)	U.S. Forest Service (FS)—Southern Research Station (SRS)	Asheville	NC	GOGO	Environmental
Dept. of Agriculture (USDA)	USDA Agricultural Research Service (ARS)—Midwest Area	Peoria	IL	GOGO	Life Sciences
Dept. of Agriculture (USDA)	USDA Agricultural Research Service (ARS)—Northeast Area	Beltsville	MD	GOGO	Life Sciences

145

Dept. of Agriculture (USDA)	USDA Agricultural Research Service (ARS) – Pacific West Area	Albany	CA	GOGO	Life Sciences
Dept. of Agriculture (USDA)	USDA Agricultural Research Service (ARS) – Plains Area	Fort Collins	TX	GOGO	Life Sciences
Dept. of Agriculture (USDA)	USDA Agricultural Research Service (ARS) – Southeast Area	Stoneville	MS	GOGO	Marine
Dept. of Agriculture (USDA)	USDA National Wildlife Research Center (NWRC)	Fort Collins	CO	GOGO	Environmental
Dept. of Commerce	Boulder Laboratories (NIST)	Boulder	CO	GOGO	Manufacturing
Dept. of Commerce	National Cybersecurity Center of Excellence (NIST)	Rockville	MD	GOCO/FFRDC	Security
Dept. of Commerce	National Institute of Standards and Technology—NIST	Gaithersburg	MD	GOGO	Electronics & Hardware
Dept. of Commerce	National Oceanic and Atmospheric Administration (NOAA)—Air Resources Laboratory	College Park	MD	GOGO	Weather
Dept. of Commerce	National Oceanic and Atmospheric Administration (NOAA)—Alaska Fisheries Science Center	Seattle	WA	GOGO	Marine
Dept. of Commerce	National Oceanic and Atmospheric Administration (NOAA)—Atlantic Oceanographic & Meteorological Laboratory	Miami	FL	GOGO	Marine

(Continued)

TABLE D-1 Continued

Agency	Name	City	State	Type	Focus
Dept. of Commerce	National Oceanic and Atmospheric Administration (NOAA)—Center for Coastal Environmental Health and Biomolecular Research	Charleston	SC	GOGO	Marine
Dept. of Commerce	National Oceanic and Atmospheric Administration (NOAA)—Center for Coastal Fisheries and Habitat Research	Beaufort	NC	GOGO	Marine
Dept. of Commerce	National Oceanic and Atmospheric Administration (NOAA)—Center for Coastal Monitoring and Assessment	Silver Spring	MD	GOGO	Marine
Dept. of Commerce	National Oceanic and Atmospheric Administration (NOAA)—Center for Satellite Applications and Research	College Park	MD	GOGO	Marine
Dept. of Commerce	National Oceanic And Atmospheric Administration (NOAA)—Earth System Research Laboratory	Boulder	CO	GOGO	Weather
Dept. of Commerce	National Oceanic and Atmospheric Administration (NOAA)—Geophysical Fluid Dynamics Laboratory	Princeton	NJ	GOGO	Environmental
Dept. of Commerce	National Oceanic and Atmospheric Administration (NOAA)—Great Lakes Environmental Research Laboratory	Ann Arbor	MI	GOGO	Marine

Dept. of Commerce	National Oceanic and Atmospheric Administration (NOAA)—Hollings Marine Laboratory	Charleston	SC	GOGO	Environmental
Dept. of Commerce	National Oceanic and Atmospheric Administration (NOAA)—Meteorological Development Laboratory	Silver Spring	MD	GOGO	Marine
Dept. of Commerce	National Oceanic and Atmospheric Administration (NOAA)—National Centers for Coastal Ocean Science (NCCOS)	Silver Spring	MD	GOGO	Marine
Dept. of Commerce	National Oceanic and Atmospheric Administration (NOAA)—National Centers for Environmental Information	Ashville	CO	GOGO	Marine
Dept. of Commerce	National Oceanic and Atmospheric Administration (NOAA)—National Centers for Environmental Prediction	College Park	MD	GOGO	Marine
Dept. of Commerce	National Oceanic and Atmospheric Administration (NOAA)—National Climatic Data Center	Asheville	NC	GOGO	Weather
Dept. of Commerce	National Oceanic and Atmospheric Administration (NOAA)—National Data Buoy Center	Stennis Space Center	MS	GOGO	Environmental

(Continued)

TABLE D-1 Continued

Agency	Name	City	State	Type	Focus
Dept. of Commerce	National Oceanic and Atmospheric Administration (NOAA)—National Geophysical Data Center	Boulder	CO	GOGO	Environmental
Dept. of Commerce	National Oceanic and Atmospheric Administration (NOAA)—National Oceanic Data Center	Silver Spring	MD	GOGO	Marine
Dept. of Commerce	National Oceanic and Atmospheric Administration (NOAA)—National Severe Storms Laboratory	Norman	OK	GOGO	Environmental
Dept. of Commerce	National Oceanic and Atmospheric Administration (NOAA)—NEXRAD Radar Operations Center	Norman	OK	GOGO	Weather
Dept. of Commerce	National Oceanic and Atmospheric Administration (NOAA)—Northeast Fisheries Science Center	Woods Hole	MA	GOGO	Marine
Dept. of Commerce	National Oceanic and Atmospheric Administration (NOAA)—Northwest Fisheries Science Center	Seattle	WA	GOGO	Environmental
Dept. of Commerce	National Oceanic and Atmospheric Administration (NOAA)—Office of Aquaculture	Silver Spring	MD	GOGO	Environmental
Dept. of Commerce	National Oceanic and Atmospheric Administration (NOAA)—Pacific Island Fisheries Science Center	Honolulu	HI	GOGO	Environmental

Dept. of Commerce	National Oceanic and Atmospheric Administration (NOAA)—Pacific Marine Environmental Laboratory	Seattle	WA	GOGO	Marine
Dept. of Commerce	National Oceanic and Atmospheric Administration (NOAA)—Southeast Fisheries Science Center	Miami	FL	GOGO	Environmental
Dept. of Commerce	National Oceanic and Atmospheric Administration (NOAA)—Southwest Fisheries Science Center	La Jolla	CA	GOGO	Environmental
Dept. of Commerce	National Oceanic and Atmospheric Administration (NOAA) Headquarters	Washington	DC	GOGO	Environmental; Marine; Weather
Dept. of Commerce	National Telecommunications and Information Administration (NTIA)	Boulder	CO	GOGO	Communications
Dept. of Defense	25th Air Force	San Antonio	TX	GOGO	Defense
Dept. of Defense	557th Weather Wing	Offutt AFB	NE	GOGO	Weather
Dept. of Defense	59th Medical Wing/ST	Joint Base San Antonio-Lackland	TX	GOGO	Medical-Health

(Continued)

TABLE D-1 Continued

Agency	Name	City	State	Type	Focus
Dept. of Defense	688th Cyberspace Wing (ACC)	JBSA Lackland	TX	GOGO	Aerospace
Dept. of Defense	Aberdeen Test Center (ATC)	Aberdeen Proving Ground	MD	GOGO	Defense
Dept. of Defense	The Aerospace Corporation	El Segundo	CA	GOCO/FFRDC	Aerospace; Defense; Electronics & Hardware; IT-Software
Dept. of Defense	Air Combat Command (ACC)	Langley AFB	VA	GOGO	Defense
Dept. of Defense	Air Force—311th Human Systems Wing	Brooks City-Base	TX	GOGO	Aerospace
Dept. of Defense	Air Force—Aeronautical Systems Center (ASC)	Wright-Patterson AFB	OH	GOGO	Defense
Dept. of Defense	Air Force 557th Weather Wing	Offutt AFB	NE	GOGO	Weather
Dept. of Defense	Air Force Academy (USAFA)	USAF Academy	CO	GOGO	Materials
Dept. of Defense	Air Force Center for Environmental Excellence (AFCEE)	Brooks City-Base	TX	GOGO	Physical Sciences
Dept. of Defense	Air Force Civil Engineer Support Agency (AFCESA)	Tyndall AFB	FL	GOGO	Physical Sciences

Dept. of Defense	Air Force Institute of Technology (AFIT)	Wright-Patterson AFB	OH	GOGO	Education
Dept. of Defense	Air Force Intelligence, Surveillance and Reconnaissance Agency (AFISRA)	JBSA Lackland	TX	GOGO	Defense
Dept. of Defense	Air Force Logistics Management Agency (AFLMA)	Maxwell AFB	AL	GOGO	Defense
Dept. of Defense	Air Force Research Laboratory (AFRL)	Wright-Patterson AFB	OH	GOGO	Aerospace
Dept. of Defense	Air Force Research Laboratory (AFRL)—711th Human Performance Wing	Wright Patterson AFB	OH	GOGO	Athletic & Performance Enhancing; Defense
Dept. of Defense	Air Force Research Laboratory (AFRL)—Aerospace Systems Directorate	Wright-Patterson AFB	OH	GOGO	Aerospace
Dept. of Defense	Air Force Research Laboratory (AFRL)—Air Force Office of Scientific Research	Arlington	VA	GOGO	Education

(Continued)

TABLE D-1 Continued

Agency	Name	City	State	Type	Focus
Dept. of Defense	Air Force Research Laboratory (AFRL)—Air Vehicles Directorate	Wright-Patterson AFB	OH	GOGO	Electronics & Hardware
Dept. of Defense	Air Force Research Laboratory (AFRL)—Directed Energy Directorate	Kirtland AFB	NM	GOGO	IT-Software
Dept. of Defense	Air Force Research Laboratory (AFRL)—Information Directorate	Rome	NY	GOGO	Aerospace
Dept. of Defense	Air Force Research Laboratory (AFRL)—Materials and Manufacturing Directorate	Wright-Patterson AFB	OH	GOGO	Manufacturing
Dept. of Defense	Air Force Research Laboratory (AFRL)—Munitions Directorate	Eglin AFB	FL	GOGO	Defense
Dept. of Defense	Air Force Research Laboratory (AFRL)—Sensors Directorate	Wright-Patterson AFB	OH	GOGO	Defense
Dept. of Defense	Air Force Research Laboratory (AFRL)—Space Vehicles Directorate—Hanscom AFB	Albuquerque	NM	GOGO	Defense
Dept. of Defense	Air Force Research Laboratory (AFRL)—Space Vehicles Directorate—Kirtland AFB	Kirtland AFB	NM	GOGO	Aerospace
Dept. of Defense	Air Force Test Center (AFTC)	Edwards AFB	CA	GOGO	Defense
Dept. of Defense	Air Mobility Battlelab (AFAMB)	Fort Dix	NJ	GOGO	Aerospace

Dept. of Defense	Army Medical Department (AMEDD) Center for Strategic Studies (CASS)	Ft. Sam Houston	TX	GOGO	Education
Dept. of Defense	Army Research Institute (ARI) for Behavioral and Social Sciences	Fort Belvoir	VA	GOGO	Education
Dept. of Defense	Army Research Laboratory (ARL)	Aberdeen Proving Ground	MD	GOGO	Education
Dept. of Defense	Arnold Engineering Development Center (AEDC)	Arnold AFB	TN	GOGO	Aerospace
Dept. of Defense	Arroyo Center	Santa Monica	CA	GOCO/FFRDC	Defense
Dept. of Defense	Benet Laboratories	Watervliet	NY	GOGO	IT-Software
Dept. of Defense	CCDC—Aviation & Missile Center—Aeroflightdynamics Directorate	Moffett Field	CA	GOGO	Defense
Dept. of Defense	CCDC—Aviation & Missile Center—Aviation Applied Technology Directorate	Ft. Eustis	VA	GOGO	Physical Sciences
Dept. of Defense	CCDC—C5ISR Center	APG	MD	GOGO	Defense
Dept. of Defense	CCDC Armaments Center	Picatinny Arsenal	NJ	GOGO	Defense
Dept. of Defense	CCDC Aviation & Missile Center	Redstone Arsenal	AL	GOGO	Aerospace
Dept. of Defense	CCDC Ground Vehicle Systems Center	Warren	MI	GOGO	Defense

(Continued)

TABLE D-1 Continued

Agency	Name	City	State	Type	Focus
Dept. of Defense	CCDC Soldier Center	Natick	MA	GOGO	Materials
Dept. of Defense	CDID Experimentation Division Network Battle Lab	Fort Gordon	GA	GOGO	Communications
Dept. of Defense	Center for Communications and Computing	Alexandria	VA	GOCO/FFRDC	Communications
Dept. of Defense	Center for Naval Analyses	Arlington	VA	GOCO/FFRDC	Defense
Dept. of Defense	Defense Advanced Research Projects Agency (DARPA)	Arlington	VA	GOGO	Defense
Dept. of Defense	Defense Language Institute Foreign Language Center (DLIFLC)	Monterey	CA	GOGO	Education
Dept. of Defense	Defense Microelectronics Activity (DMEA)	McClellan	CA	GOGO	Defense
Dept. of Defense	Defense Technical Information Center (DTIC)	Fort Belvoir	VA	GOGO	Defense
Dept. of Defense	DISA—Joint Interoperability Test Command (JITC)	Indian Head	MD	GOGO	Communications
Dept. of Defense	Dugway Proving Ground (DPG)	Dugway	UT	GOGO	Defense
Dept. of Defense	Electronic Systems Center (ESC)	Hanscom AFB	MA	GOGO	Communications
Dept. of Defense	Engineer Research and Development Center (ERDC)	Vicksburg	MS	GOGO	Defense
Dept. of Defense	ERDC-Geospatial Research Laboratory	Vicksburg	MS	GOGO	Defense

155

Dept. of Defense	Federal U-2 Laboratory	Beale AFB	CA	GOGO	Aerospace; Defense; Electronics & Hardware; IT-Software
Dept. of Defense	Fleet Readiness Center (FRC) East—Vertical Lift Center of Excellence	Cherry Point	NC	GOGO	Energy
Dept. of Defense	Fleet Readiness Center Southeast (FRCSE)	Jacksonville	FL	GOGO	Materials
Dept. of Defense	Fleet Readiness Center Southwest (FRCSW)	San Diego	CA	GOGO	Defense
Dept. of Defense	Headquarters United States Marine Corps Intelligence Department	Quantico	VA	GOGO	Defense
Dept. of Defense	Laser Facility, Bldg A4	San Diego	CA	GOGO	Electronics & Hardware
Dept. of Defense	Marine Corps Cyberspace Operations Group	Quantico	VA	GOGO	IT-Software
Dept. of Defense	Marine Corps Installations West	Camp Pendleton	CA	GOGO	Defense
Dept. of Defense	Marine Corps Systems Command (MCSC)	Quantico	VA	GOGO	Defense
Dept. of Defense	Missile Defense Agency (MDA)	Washington	DC	GOGO	Defense
Dept. of Defense	MIT Lincoln Laboratory	Lexington	MA	GOCO/FFRDC	Electronics & Hardware
Dept. of Defense	National Defense Research Institute	Santa Monica	CA	GOCO/FFRDC	Defense

(Continued)

TABLE D-1 Continued

Agency	Name	City	State	Type	Focus
Dept. of Defense	National Geospatial-Intelligence Agency (NGA)	Springfield	VA	GOGO	Communications
Dept. of Defense	National Naval Medical Center	Bethesda	MD	GOGO	Medical-Health
Dept. of Defense	National Security Agency (NSA) Technology Transfer Program	Ft. Meade	MD	GOGO	Security
Dept. of Defense	National Security Engineering Center	Bedford	MA	GOCO/FFRDC	Security
Dept. of Defense	Naval Aerospace Medical Research Laboratory (NAMRL)	Pensacola	FL	GOGO	Medical-Health
Dept. of Defense	Naval Air Systems Command	Patuxent River	MD	GOGO	Aerospace
Dept. of Defense	Naval Air Warfare Center—Weapons Division—China Lake and Pt. Mugu	China Lake	CA	GOGO	Aerospace
Dept. of Defense	Naval Air Warfare Center (NAWC)—Aircraft Division—Lakehurst	Lakehurst	NJ	GOGO	Materials
Dept. of Defense	Naval Air Warfare Center (NAWC)—Aircraft Division—Patuxent River	Patuxent River	MD	GOGO	Aerospace
Dept. of Defense	Naval Air Warfare Center Training Systems Division (NAWCTSD)	Orlando	FL	GOGO	Aerospace
Dept. of Defense	Naval Entomology Center of Excellence	Jacksonville	FL	GOGO	Life Sciences
Dept. of Defense	Naval Explosive Ordnance Disposal Technology Division	Indian Head	MD	GOGO	Defense

Dept. of Defense	Naval Facilities Engineering and Expeditionary Warfare Center (NAVFAC EXWC)	Port Hueneme	CA	GOGO	Defense
Dept. of Defense	Naval Health Research Center (NHRC)	San Diego	CA	GOGO	Medical-Health
Dept. of Defense	Naval Information Warfare Center, Pacific (NIWC)	San Diego	CA	GOGO	Defense
Dept. of Defense	Naval Information Warfare Centers (NIWC), Atlantic	North Charleston	SC	GOGO	Defense
Dept. of Defense	Naval Medical Center—Portsmouth	Portsmouth	VA	GOGO	Medical-Health
Dept. of Defense	Naval Medical Center—San Diego (NMCSD)	San Diego	CA	GOGO	Medical-Health
Dept. of Defense	Naval Medical Research Center	Silver Spring	MD	GOGO	Medical-Health
Dept. of Defense	Naval Medical Research Unit—Dayton	Wright Patterson AFB	OH	GOGO	Medical-Health
Dept. of Defense	Naval Medical Research Unit—San Antonio	Fort Sam Houston	TX	GOGO	Medical-Health
Dept. of Defense	Naval Meteorology and Oceanography Command (NAVMETOCCOM)	Stennis Space Center	MS	GOGO	Environmental; Marine; Weather
Dept. of Defense	Naval Postgraduate School	Monterey	CA	GOGO	Education
Dept. of Defense	Naval Safety Center	Norfolk	VA	GOGO	Defense

(Continued)

TABLE D-1 Continued

Agency	Name	City	State	Type	Focus
Dept. of Defense	Naval Submarine Medical Research Laboratory (NSMRL)	Groton	CT	GOGO	Medical-Health
Dept. of Defense	Naval Surface Warfare Center—Carderock Division (NSWCCD)—Naval Ship Systems Engineering Station	Philadelphia	PA	GOGO	Defense
Dept. of Defense	Naval Surface Warfare Center (NSWC)—Carderock Division	West Bethesda	MD	GOGO	Defense
Dept. of Defense	Naval Surface Warfare Center (NSWC)—Corona Division	Corona	CA	GOGO	Defense
Dept. of Defense	Naval Surface Warfare Center (NSWC)—Crane Division	Crane	IN	GOGO	Defense
Dept. of Defense	Naval Surface Warfare Center (NSWC)—Dahlgren Division (NSWCDD)	Dahlgren	VA	GOGO	Defense
Dept. of Defense	Naval Surface Warfare Center (NSWC)—Indian Head Explosive Ordnance Disposal Technology Division	Indian Head	MD	GOGO	Materials
Dept. of Defense	Naval Surface Warfare Center (NSWC)—NAVSEA Port Hueneme Division	Port Hueneme	CA	GOGO	Physical Sciences
Dept. of Defense	Naval Surface Warfare Center (NSWC)—Panama City Division	Panama City	FL	GOGO	Defense
Dept. of Defense	Naval Undersea Warfare Center (NUWC)—Division Keyport	Keyport	WA	GOGO	Physical Sciences

Dept. of Defense	Naval Undersea Warfare Center (NUWC)—Division Newport	Newport	RI	GOGO	Physical Sciences
Dept. of Defense	Naval War College (NWC)	Newport	RI	GOGO	Education
Dept. of Defense	NAVSEA Portsmouth Naval Shipyard	Portsmouth	NH	GOGO	Defense
Dept. of Defense	Navy Clothing and Textile Research Facility (NCRTF)	Natick	MA	GOGO	Materials
Dept. of Defense	Navy Warfare Development Command (NWDC)	Norfolk	VA	GOGO	Education
Dept. of Defense	Norfolk Naval Shipyard	Portsmouth	VA	GOGO	Defense
Dept. of Defense	Office of Naval Research (ONR)	Arlington	VA	GOGO	Defense
Dept. of Defense	Ogden Air Logistics Center (ALC)	Hill AFB	UT	GOGO	Defense
Dept. of Defense	Oklahoma City Air Logistics Center (ALC)	Tinker AFB	OK	GOGO	Aerospace
Dept. of Defense	Pearl Harbor Naval Shipyard & Intermediate Maintenance Facility	Joint Base Pearl Harbor-Hickam	HI	GOGO	Marine
Dept. of Defense	Project Air Force	Santa Monica	CA	GOCO/FFRDC	Defense
Dept. of Defense	Puget Sound Naval Shipyard & Intermediate Maintenance Facility	Bremerton	WA	GOGO	Defense
Dept. of Defense	RDECOM—Simulation and Training Technology Center	Orlando	FL	GOGO	Defense
Dept. of Defense	Redstone Test Center (RTC)	Redstone Arsenal	AL	GOGO	Weather

(Continued)

TABLE D-1 Continued

Agency	Name	City	State	Type	Focus
Dept. of Defense	Software Engineering Institute	Pittsburgh	PA	GOCO/FFRDC	IT-Software
Dept. of Defense	Systems and Analyses Center	Alexandria	VA	GOCO/FFRDC	Defense
Dept. of Defense	The Defense Health Agency (DHA)	Falls Church	VA	GOGO	Medical-Health
Dept. of Defense	U.S. Army Center for Environmental Health Research	Fort Detrick	MD	GOGO	Medical-Health
Dept. of Defense	U.S. Army Clinical Investigation Regulatory Office	Ft. Detrick	MD	GOGO	Medical-Health
Dept. of Defense	U.S. Army Combat Capabilities Development Command Chemical Biological Center	Aberdeen Proving Ground	MD	GOGO	Security
Dept. of Defense	U.S. Army Developmental Test Command (DTC)	Aberdeen Proving Ground	MD	GOGO	Defense
Dept. of Defense	U.S. Army Electronic Proving Ground	Ft. Huachuca	AZ	GOGO	Communications
Dept. of Defense	U.S. Army Institute of Surgical Research (USAISR)	Ft. Sam Houston	TX	GOGO	Medical-Health
Dept. of Defense	U.S. Army Medical Materiel Development Activity (USAMMDA)	Fort Detrick	MD	GOGO	Medical-Health
Dept. of Defense	U.S. Army Medical Research & Development Command—Medical Technology Transfer Office (MTT)	Fort Detrick	MD	GOGO	Medical-Health

Dept. of Defense	U.S. Army Medical Research Institute of Chemical Defense (USAMRICD)	Aberdeen Proving Ground	MD	GOGO	Medical-Health
Dept. of Defense	U.S. Army Medical Research Institute of Infectious Diseases (USAMRIID)	Ft. Detrick	MD	GOGO	Medical-Health
Dept. of Defense	U.S. Army Research Institute of Environmental Medicine (USARIEM)	Natick	MA	GOGO	Athletic & Performance Enhancing; Medical-Health
Dept. of Defense	U.S. Army Space and Missile Defense Command/Army Forces Strategic Command (USASMDC/ARSTRAT)	Huntsville	AL	GOGO	Aerospace; Defense; Electronics & Hardware; IT-Software
Dept. of Defense	U.S. Army TRADOC Analysis Center (TRAC)	Fort Leavenworth	KS	GOGO	Defense
Dept. of Defense	U.S. Joint Forces Command (USJFCOM)	Norfolk	VA	GOGO	Defense
Dept. of Defense	U.S. Marine Corps Forces Cyberspace Command	Fort George G. Meade	MD	GOGO	Defense
Dept. of Defense	U.S. Naval Observatory (USNO)	Washington	DC	GOGO	Communications
Dept. of Defense	U.S. Naval Research Laboratory (NRL)	Washington	DC	GOGO	IT-Software
Dept. of Defense	U.S. Transportation Command (USTRANSCOM)	Scott AFB	IL	GOGO	Transportation

(Continued)

TABLE D-1 Continued

Agency	Name	City	State	Type	Focus
Dept. of Defense	Uniformed Services University of the Health Services (USUHS)	Bethesda	MD	GOGO	Medical-Health
Dept. of Defense	United States Naval Academy	Annapolis	MD	GOGO	Education
Dept. of Defense	US Army Aeromedical Research Laboratory (USAARL)	Fort Rucker	AL	GOGO	Athletic & Performance Enhancing; Defense
Dept. of Defense	USACE—ERDC—Coastal and Hydraulics Laboratory	Vicksburg	MS	GOGO	Physical Sciences
Dept. of Defense	USACE—ERDC—Cold Regions Research and Engineering Laboratory	Hanover	NH	GOGO	Physical Sciences
Dept. of Defense	USACE—ERDC—Construction Engineering Research Laboratory	Champaign	IL	GOGO	Physical Sciences
Dept. of Defense	USACE—ERDC—Environmental Laboratory	Vicksburg	MS	GOGO	Environmental
Dept. of Defense	USACE—ERDC—Geotechnical and Structures Laboratory	Vicksburg	MS	GOGO	Materials
Dept. of Defense	USACE—ERDC—Information Technology Laboratory	Vicksburg	MS	GOGO	Physical Sciences
Dept. of Defense	USACE—Institute for Water Resources	Alexandria	VA	GOGO	Environmental

163

					Athletic & Performance Enhancing; Medical-Health
Dept. of Defense	USAMRMC—Telemedicine and Advanced Technology Research Center	Ft. Detrick	MD	GOGO	
Dept. of Defense	Walter Reed Army Institute of Research (WRAIR)	Silver Spring	MD	GOGO	Defense
Dept. of Defense	Warner Robins Air Logistics Complex (WRALC)	Robins AFB	GA	GOGO	Defense
Dept. of Defense	Yuma Proving Ground (USAYPG)	Yuma	AZ	GOGO	Defense
Dept. of Energy	Ames Laboratory (AL)	Ames	IA	GOCO/FFRDC	Energy
Dept. of Energy	Argonne National Laboratory (ANL)	Argonne	IL	GOCO/FFRDC	Physical Sciences
Dept. of Energy	Brookhaven National Laboratory (BNL)	Upton	NY	GOCO/FFRDC	Energy
Dept. of Energy	Fermi National Accelerator Laboratory (FNAL)	Batavia	IL	GOCO/FFRDC	Energy
Dept. of Energy	Idaho National Laboratory (INL)	Idaho Falls	ID	GOCO/FFRDC	Nuclear
Dept. of Energy	Kansas City National Security Campus	Kansas City	MO	GOCO	Defense
Dept. of Energy	Lawrence Berkeley National Laboratory (LBNL)	Berkeley	CA	GOCO/FFRDC	Education
Dept. of Energy	Lawrence Livermore National Laboratory (LLNL)	Livermore	CA	GOCO/FFRDC	Materials
Dept. of Energy	Los Alamos National Laboratory (LANL)	Los Alamos	NM	GOCO/FFRDC	Materials

(Continued)

TABLE D-1 Continued

Agency	Name	City	State	Type	Focus
Dept. of Energy	National Energy Technology Laboratory (NETL)—Albany, OR	Albany	OR	GOGO	Energy
Dept. of Energy	National Energy Technology Laboratory (NETL)—Fairbanks, AK	Fairbanks	AK	GOGO	Energy
Dept. of Energy	National Energy Technology Laboratory (NETL)—Houston, TX	Houston	TX	GOGO	Energy
Dept. of Energy	National Energy Technology Laboratory (NETL)—Morgantown, WV	Morgantown	WV	GOGO	Energy
Dept. of Energy	National Energy Technology Laboratory (NETL)—Pittsburgh, PA	Pittsburgh	PA	GOGO	Energy
Dept. of Energy	National Nuclear Security Administration (NNSA)—Pantex Plant	Amarillo	TX	GOCO	Physical Sciences
Dept. of Energy	National Renewable Energy Laboratory (NREL)	Golden	CO	GOCO/FFRDC	Energy
Dept. of Energy	Oak Ridge National Laboratory (ORNL)	Oak Ridge	TN	GOCO/FFRDC	Environmental
Dept. of Energy	Pacific Northwest National Laboratory (PNNL)	Richland	WA	GOCO/FFRDC	Energy
Dept. of Energy	Princeton Plasma Physics Laboratory (PPPL)	Princeton	NJ	GOCO/FFRDC	Nuclear
Dept. of Energy	Sandia National Laboratories—California	Livermore	CA	GOCO/FFRDC	Energy
Dept. of Energy	Sandia National Laboratories (SNL)	Albuquerque	NM	GOCO/FFRDC	Energy
Dept. of Energy	Savannah River National Laboratory (SRNL)	Aiken	SC	GOCO/FFRDC	Security
Dept. of Energy	SLAC National Accelerator Laboratory	Menlo Park	CA	GOCO/FFRDC	Physical Sciences

Dept. of Energy	Thomas Jefferson National Accelerator Facility (Jefferson Lab)	Newport News	VA	GOCO/FFRDC	Nuclear
Dept. of Energy	U.S. Department of Energy (DOE)—Hanford Site	Richland	WA	GOCO	Energy
Dept. of Energy	Y-12 National Security Complex	Oak Ridge	TN	GOCO	Manufacturing
Dept. of Health and Human Services	Center for Drug Evaluation and Research (CDER)	Silver Spring	MD	GOGO	Medical-Health
Dept. of Health and Human Services	Center for Information Technology (CIT)	Bethesda	MD	GOGO	IT-Software
Dept. of Health and Human Services	Center for Medicare & Medicaid Services—Alliance to Modernize Healthcare	Baltimore	MD	GOCO/FFRDC	Medical-Health
Dept. of Health and Human Services	Center for Tobacco Products (CTP)	Silver Spring	MD	GOGO	Medical-Health
Dept. of Health and Human Services	Center for Veterinary Medicine (CVM)	Rockville	MD	GOGO	Medical-Health
Dept. of Health and Human Services	Centers for Disease Control and Prevention (CDC)	Atlanta	GA	GOGO	Medical-Health
Dept. of Health and Human Services	Clinical Center at the National Institutes of Health (NIH)	Bethesda	MD	GOGO	Medical-Health

(Continued)

TABLE D-1 Continued

Agency	Name	City	State	Type	Focus
Dept. of Health and Human Services	Fogarty International Center (FICNIH)	Bethesda	MD	GOGO	Medical-Health
Dept. of Health and Human Services	Frederick National Laboratory for Cancer Research	Frederick	MD	GOCO/FFRDC	Medical-Health
Dept. of Health and Human Services	National Cancer Institute (NCI)	Bethesda	MD	GOGO	Medical-Health
Dept. of Health and Human Services	National Center for Advancing Translational Sciences (NCATS)	Rockville	MD	GOGO	Medical-Health
Dept. of Health and Human Services	National Center for Complementary and Alternative Medicine (NCCAM)	Bethesda	MD	GOGO	Medical-Health
Dept. of Health and Human Services	National Center for Research Resources (NCRR)	Bethesda	MD	GOGO	Medical-Health
Dept. of Health and Human Services	National Center for Toxicological Research (NCTR)	Jefferson	AR	GOGO	IT-Software
Dept. of Health and Human Services	National Eye Institute (NEI)	Bethesda	MD	GOGO	Medical-Health
Dept. of Health and Human Services	National Heart, Lung, and Blood Institute (NHLBI)	Bethesda	MD	GOGO	Medical-Health

Dept. of Health and Human Services	National Human Genome Research Institute (NHGRI)	Bethesda	MD	GOGO	Medical-Health
Dept. of Health and Human Services	National Institute for Occupational Safety and Health (NIOSH)	Cincinnati	OH	GOGO	Medical-Health
Dept. of Health and Human Services	National Institute for Occupational Safety and Health (NIOSH)—Pittsburgh Research Laboratory	Pittsburgh	PA	GOGO	Medical-Health
Dept. of Health and Human Services	National Institute for Occupational Safety and Health (NIOSH)—Spokane Research Laboratory	Spokane	WA	GOGO	Medical-Health
Dept. of Health and Human Services	National Institute of Allergy and Infectious Diseases (NIAID)	Bethesda	MD	GOGO	Medical-Health
Dept. of Health and Human Services	National Institute of Arthritis and Musculoskeletal and Skin Diseases (NIAMS)	Bethesda	MD	GOGO	Medical-Health
Dept. of Health and Human Services	National Institute of Biomedical Imaging and Bioengineering (NIBIB)	Bethesda	MD	GOGO	Medical-Health
Dept. of Health and Human Services	National Institute of Child Health and Human Development (NICHD)	Bethesda	MD	GOGO	Medical-Health
Dept. of Health and Human Services	National Institute of Dental and Craniofacial Research (NIDCR)	Bethesda	MD	GOGO	Medical-Health

(Continued)

TABLE D-1 Continued

Agency	Name	City	State	Type	Focus
Dept. of Health and Human Services	National Institute of Diabetes and Digestive and Kidney Diseases (NIDDK)	Bethesda	MD	GOGO	Medical-Health
Dept. of Health and Human Services	National Institute of Environmental Health Sciences (NIEHS)	Research Triangle Park	NC	GOGO	Medical-Health
Dept. of Health and Human Services	National Institute of General Medical Sciences (NIGMS)	Bethesda	MD	GOGO	Medical-Health
Dept. of Health and Human Services	National Institute of Mental Health (NIMH)	Bethesda	MD	GOGO	Medical-Health
Dept. of Health and Human Services	National Institute of Neurological Disorders and Stroke (NINDS)	Bethesda	MD	GOGO	Medical-Health
Dept. of Health and Human Services	National Institute of Nursing Research (NINR)	Bethesda	MD	GOGO	Medical-Health
Dept. of Health and Human Services	National Institute on Aging (NIA)	Bethesda	MD	GOGO	Medical-Health
Dept. of Health and Human Services	National Institute on Alcohol Abuse and Alcoholism (NIAAA)	Bethesda	MD	GOGO	Medical-Health
Dept. of Health and Human Services	National Institute on Deafness and Other Communication Disorders (NIDCD)	Bethesda	MD	GOGO	Medical-Health

Dept. of Health and Human Services	National Institute on Drug Abuse (NIDA)	Bethesda	MD	GOGO	Medical-Health
Dept. of Health and Human Services	National Institutes of Health (NIH)	Rockville	MD	GOGO	Medical-Health
Dept. of Health and Human Services	National Library of Medicine (NLM)	Bethesda	MD	GOGO	Medical-Health
Dept. of Health and Human Services	Office of Infectious Diseases (OID)	Atlanta	GA	GOGO	Medical-Health
Dept. of Health and Human Services	Office of Regulatory Affairs (ORA)	Silver Spring	MD	GOGO	Medical-Health
Dept. of Health and Human Services	Office of Research Services (ORS)	Bethesda	MD	GOGO	Security
Dept. of Health and Human Services	U.S. Food and Drug Administration (FDA)	Silver Spring	MD	GOGO	Medical-Health
Dept. of Health and Human Services	U.S. Food and Drug Administration (FDA)—Center for Biologics Evaluation and Research (CBER)	Rockville	MD	GOGO	Medical-Health
Dept. of Health and Human Services	U.S. Food and Drug Administration (FDA)—Center for Devices and Radiological Health (CDRH)	Silver Spring	MD	GOGO	Medical-Health

(Continued)

TABLE D-1 Continued

Agency	Name	City	State	Type	Focus
Dept. of Health and Human Services	U.S. Food and Drug Administration (FDA)—Center for Food Safety and Applied Nutrition (CFSAN)	Washington	DC	GOGO	Medical-Health
Dept. of Homeland Security	Chemical Security Analysis Center (CSAC)	Aberdeen Proving Ground	MD	GOGO	Physical Sciences
Dept. of Homeland Security	Federal Law Enforcement Training Center (FLETC)	Glynco	GA	GOGO	Security
Dept. of Homeland Security	Homeland Security Operational Analysis Center	Pentagon City	VA	GOCO/FFRDC	Security
Dept. of Homeland Security	Homeland Security Systems Engineering and Development Institute	McLean	VA	GOCO/FFRDC	Security
Dept. of Homeland Security	National Biodefense Analysis and Countermeasures Center (NBACC)	Frederick	MD	GOCO/FFRDC	Life Sciences
Dept. of Homeland Security	National Urban Security Technology Laboratory (NUSTL)	New York	NY	GOGO	Security
Dept. of Homeland Security	Plum Island Animal Disease Center (PIADC)	Greenport	NY	GOGO	Medical-Health
Dept. of Homeland Security	Transportation Security Laboratory (TSL)	Atlantic City International Airport	NJ	GOGO	Transportation

Dept. of Homeland Security	U.S. Coast Guard Research and Development Center	New London	CT	GOGO	Defense
Dept. of Interior	Bureau of Reclamation (BR)	Denver	CO	GOGO	Environmental
Dept. of Interior	Defense Centers of Excellence	Silver Spring	MD	GOGO	Defense
Dept. of Interior	Great Lakes Science Center	Ann Arbor	MI	GOGO	Marine
Dept. of Interior	Northern Prairie Wildlife Research Center (NPWRC)	Jamestown	ND	GOGO	Environmental
Dept. of Interior	USGS National Labs	Reston	VA	GOGO	Energy; Environmental; Physical Sciences
Dept. of Labor	Mine Safety and Health Administration (MSHA)	Arlington	VA	GOGO	Medical-Health
Dept. of the Treasury	Center for Enterprise Modernization	McLean	VA	GOCO/FFRDC	IT-Software
Dept. of Transportation	Center for Advanced Aviation System Development	McLean	VA	GOCO/FFRDC	Transportation
Dept. of Transportation	Federal Aviation Administration	Washington	DC	GOGO	Aerospace
Dept. of Transportation	Federal Aviation Administration (FAA)—Civil Aerospace Medical Institute	Oklahoma City	OK	GOGO	Medical-Health
Dept. of Transportation	Federal Aviation Administration (FAA)—William J. Hughes Technical Center (WJHTC)	Egg Harbor Township	NJ	GOGO	Aerospace

(Continued)

171

TABLE D-1 Continued

Agency	Name	City	State	Type	Focus
Dept. of Transportation	Federal Highway Administration (FHWA)—Turner-Fairbank Highway Research Center (TFHRC)	McLean	VA	GOGO	Transportation
Dept. of Transportation	Federal Railroad Administration—Transportation Technology Center (TTC)	Pueblo	CO	GOGO	Transportation
Dept. of Transportation	John A. Volpe National Transportation Systems Center (Volpe Center)	Cambridge	MA	GOGO	Transportation
Dept. of Transportation	U.S. Maritime Administration	Washington	DC	GOGO	Marine
Dept. of Veterans Affairs	Department of Veterans Affairs, Office of Research and Development (VA)	Washington	DC	GOGO	Medical-Health
Environmental Protection Agency	Environmental Protection Laboratories	Ft. Meade	MD	GOGO	Environmental
Environmental Protection Agency	National Center for Computational Toxicology (NCCT)	Research Triangle Park	NC	GOGO	IT-Software
Environmental Protection Agency	National Center for Environmental Research (NCER)	Washington	DC	GOGO	Environmental
Environmental Protection Agency	National Exposure Research Laboratory (NERL)	Research Triangle Park	NC	GOGO	Medical-Health
Environmental Protection Agency	National Health and Environmental Effects Research Laboratory (NHEERL)	Research Triangle Park	NC	GOGO	Medical-Health

Environmental Protection Agency	National Homeland Security Research Center (NHSRC)	Cincinnati	OH	GOGO	Defense
Environmental Protection Agency	National Risk Management Research Laboratory (NRMRL)	Cincinnati	OH	GOGO	Environmental
Environmental Protection Agency	Office of Science Policy (OSP)	Washington	DC	GOGO	Environmental
National Aeronautics and Space Administration	NASA Ames Research Center	Moffett Field	CA	GOGO	Aerospace
National Aeronautics and Space Administration	NASA Armstrong Flight Research Center	Edwards	CA	GOGO	Aerospace
National Aeronautics and Space Administration	NASA Glenn Research Center	Cleveland	OH	GOGO	Aerospace
National Aeronautics and Space Administration	NASA Goddard Space Flight Center	Greenbelt	MD	GOGO	Aerospace
National Aeronautics and Space Administration	NASA Headquarters	Washington	DC	GOGO	Aerospace; Life Sciences
National Aeronautics and Space Administration	NASA Jet Propulsion Laboratory	Pasadena	CA	GOCO/FFRDC	Aerospace

(Continued)

TABLE D-1 Continued

Agency	Name	City	State	Type	Focus
National Aeronautics and Space Administration	NASA Johnson Space Center	Houston	TX	GOGO	Aerospace
National Aeronautics and Space Administration	NASA Kennedy Space Center	Kennedy Space Center	FL	GOGO	Aerospace
National Aeronautics and Space Administration	NASA Langley Research Center	Hampton	VA	GOGO	Aerospace
National Aeronautics and Space Administration	NASA Marshall Space Flight Center	Huntsville	AL	GOGO	Aerospace
National Aeronautics and Space Administration	NASA Stennis Space Center	Stennis Space Center	MS	GOGO	Materials
National Science Foundation	National Center for Atmospheric Research	Boulder	CO	GOCO/FFRDC	Environmental
National Science Foundation	National Optical Astronomy Observatory (NOAO)	Tucson	AZ	GOCO/FFRDC	Physical Sciences; Electronics and Hardware

National Science Foundation	National Radio Astronomy Observatory (NRAO)	Charlottesville	VA	GOCO/FFRDC	Communications; Electronics & Hardware; IT-Software; Physical Sciences
National Science Foundation	National Solar Observatory	Sunspot	NM	GOCO/FFRDC	Physical Sciences; Electronics and Hardware
National Science Foundation	Science and Technology Policy Institute	Washington	DC	GOCO/FFRDC	Education
Nuclear Regulatory Commission	Center for Nuclear Waste Regulatory Analyses	San Antonio	TX	GOCO/FFRDC	Nuclear
United States Courts	Judiciary Engineering and Modernization Center	McLean	VA	GOCO/FFRDC	Education